LEAVE IT TO BOOMER

A LOOK AT LIFE, LOVE AND PARENTHOOD BY THE VERY MODEL OF THE MODERN MIDDLE-AGE MAN

JERRY ZEZIMA

IUNIVERSE, INC.
NEW YORK   BLOOMINGTON

Leave It to Boomer
A Look at Life, Love and Parenthood by the Very
Model of the Modern Middle-Age Man

iUniverse books may be ordered through booksellers or by contacting:

iUniverse
1663 Liberty Drive
Bloomington, IN 47403
www.iuniverse.com
1-800-Authors (1-800-288-4677)

Because of the dynamic nature of the Internet, any Web addresses or links contained in this book may have changed since publication and may no longer be valid.

ISBN: 978-1-4401-9431-3 (sc)
ISBN: 978-1-4401-9432-0 (ebk)

Printed in the United States of America

iUniverse rev. date: 12/17/2009

Contents

Dedication   ix

Acknowledgments   xi

INTRODUCTION   xiii

CHAPTER 1: "CHILDREN OF A LESSER DAD"   **1**
"Why Kids Are Hard of Hearing"   1
"Parents Shouldn't Be Seen or Heard"   3
"Going for Broke With Fundraisers"   5
"In Softball, Girls Will Be Girls"   7
"Deliver Me From This Paper Route"   9
"The Yolk's on Him"   11
"How to Carve a Pumpkin"   13

CHAPTER 2: "TEENGLISH SPOKEN HERE"   **16**
"You Don't Say"   16
"Language Barrier"   18
"Driving Yourself Crazy"   19
"The Pajama Game"   21
"Road Test"   23
"Brain Drain"   26

CHAPTER 3: "COLLEGE DAZE"   **29**
"What I Learned on My College Tour"   29
"Disaster Area"   30
"Final Exam"   32
"The New Roommate"   34

"A Moving Experience" 36

CHAPTER 4: "PET PROJECTS" 39
"Taste Test Is the Cat's Meow" 39
"Love Connection" 41
"Doggie Dentistry" 43
"Mind Over Matter" 45
"A Ruff Game" 47
"Open Door Policy" 49
"Lizzie Meets Lassie" 51
"Ramona" 52

CHAPTER 5: "IT'S A GUY THING" 55
"Leaving No Stone Unpassed" 55
"A Briefing by Inspector No. 122" 57
"Uncovering Victoria's Big Holiday Secret" 59
"A Real Gem" 62
"Baby Face Zezima" 63
"Oh, Give Me a Foam Where the Beer Is My Own" 65
"I Stooge to Conquer" 67
"The Lord of the Ringtones" 69
"Bumper Cars" 71

CHAPTER 6: "DOMESTIC DILEMMAS" 74
"Someone's in the Kitchen With a Paintbrush" 74
"The Heat's On" 76
"A Real Swinger" 78
"Withering Heights" 79
"Growing Pains" 81

CHAPTER 7: "THE MIDDLE AGES" 84
"The Big 5-Oh!" 84
"One Tough Cookie" 88

CHAPTER 8: "FATHER OF THE BRIDE" 92
"Fully Engaged" 92
"Meet the Zezimas" 94
"Dancing With the Stiffs" 96
"Let Them Eat Cake" 98
"Dad Takes a Bridal Shower" 100
"Beautiful Schemer" 101

"The Big Day" 103

CHAPTER 9: "MISCELLANEOUS MUSINGS" 106
"Thanks for the Memory" 106
"Amazing Braces" 108
"The Eyes Have It" 110
"Out of Shape and Into Yoga" 112
"Web of Intrigue" 114
"Shark Dive" 115
"Show Me the Money" 117
"Jailhouse Talk" 120
"Fast Paul and the Ping-Pong Kid" 123
"A Work of Art" 125

CHAPTER 10: "SUE & JERRY'S EXCELLENT ADVENTURES" 128
"Love and Marriage" 128
"The Honeymooners" 130
"Move Over, Don Juan" 133
"Disorder in the Court" 135
"Putting on Heirs" 137
"High Roller" 138
"Home, Sweat Home" 140
"Color My World" 142
"Grape Expectations" 144
"Day at the Museum" 146
"Moby-Sick" 147
"Identity Crisis" 149
"Mr. and Mrs. Excitement" 151
"It's in the Bag" 153

EPILOGUE 155

DEDICATION

This book is dedicated to my wife, Sue, who is still my sweetheart after all these years, and to our daughters, Katie and Lauren, the apples of my eye. Thank you for filling my life with love and laughter and for putting up, if sometimes only barely, with my stupid jokes.

Acknowledgments

Let's begin at the beginning – with my parents, Rosina and Jerry Zezima Sr. Thank you for all your love, wisdom and encouragement, and for instilling in me the value of humor.

To my sisters, Elizabeth and Susan, and to Susan's family: her husband, Richard, and their children, Taylor, Blair and Whitney.

To my mother-in-law and father-in-law, Jo and Carmine Pikero; to my brother-in-law Kevin, his wife, Lynn, and their children, Andrew, Kevin and Ashley; and to my sister-in-law Cecile and her children, Jordan and Vicki.

To my son-in-law, Dave. Katie couldn't have married a better guy.

To my hometown paper, The Stamford Advocate in Connecticut, where I began my journalism career and for which I am still writing my humor column. I am forever grateful. There have been far too many friends and colleagues to acknowledge, but those who either helped me get started or have edited and championed my column include Bob Kennedy, Joyce Gabriel, Barry Hoffman, Stacy Schneider, Joe Pisani, Terri Vanech, John Breunig and especially Valerie Foster.

To the Los Angeles Times-Washington Post News Service, which has distributed my column to newspapers across the country and around the world. Thanks to Carlos Selva, Denise Bennett and the gang.

To my friends and colleagues at Newsday. Again, there are too many to acknowledge, but a special tip of the hat to Jack Millrod, Jim Smith, Robert Fouch and Ronnie Gill.

To dear friends, including the Richerts, the Lovelettes, the Hugheses and Peter Keefe.

To Robert L. Dilenschneider, for his guidance and support.

To my agent, Janet Rosen, of Sheree Bykofsky Associates, for believing in me and working so hard on my behalf. Thanks also to Sheree herself, for taking me on as a client.

To Rick Meils, Martha Rigdon, Cory Hovious and the team at iUniverse, for helping to make this book a reality.

Apologies to anyone I may have left out, but look at the bright side: Now you are not guilty by association.

INTRODUCTION

On January 11, 1954, a date which will live in infancy, I became a baby boomer. Full credit goes to my mother, Rosina, aka "Foxy Roxy," and my father, the original and by far the best Jerry Zezima. I didn't help much because I was born more than three weeks past my due date and haven't been on time for anything since.

On April 2, 1978, I became a husband. Like many of my baby boomer friends, I got married early (it was a 10 o'clock wedding). I wanted to get married on April Fool's Day, but my bride, Sue, was opposed to the idea, probably because she didn't want to receive whoopee cushions as anniversary gifts. We are, blessedly, still married.

On July 17, 1980, I became a father. A little before midnight on that humid midsummer's eve, in the stifling heat of our apartment, Sue waddled from the bedroom to the top of the stairs to announce that her water had broken and that it was time to go to the hospital.

"Just a minute," I shouted from my chair downstairs in the living room, where I was watching TV and drinking a beer. "The Three Stooges are on. The show's almost over." It was the classic episode in which Curly goes crazy when he hears "Pop Goes the Weasel."

Sue, who had already packed her bags, was about to pack mine. Fortunately for me, there wasn't time. So, as the Stooges faded to black, I whisked her into the car and sped to the hospital, where my main job, as I had learned in our Lamaze class, was to help Sue along by reminding her to perform an involuntary reflex. "Breathe," I was supposed to tell her.

Before I could be useful, an opportunity that doesn't happen every day for most men, Sue said, "I have to go to the bathroom." There, in the tiny porcelain confines, where I had to remind myself *not* to breathe, Sue almost gave birth in the toilet. It would have been the first time in the annals of medicine that a baby had been born feeling flushed. About 20 minutes later, at 3:27 a.m., Katherine Ann Zezima made her grand entrance into the world.

On November 13, 1982, I became a father again. This time, the doctor and I were watching Road Runner cartoons in the delivery room. Sue, who by now had managed to get the hang of breathing on her own, looked at me through incredulous eyes. If she had possessed a stick of dynamite from the Acme Company, she no doubt would have lighted it and handed it to me.

Sssssssssssssss ... BOOM!

Again, fortunately for me, there wasn't time. A little while later, at 10:03 a.m., Lauren Marie Zezima was born.

Sometimes I wonder how I managed to become a father whose two daughters have grown up to be wonderful, well-adjusted young women. The answer is simple: They take after their mother. And therein lies the secret: If it weren't for my wife, I would be either dead or in prison. Sue and I met when we were teenagers. We went to the same high school, we went to the same college, she wouldn't stop following me so I had to marry her.

Many people graduate from college and immediately focus on what they hope will be brilliant and successful careers. Others take time off and set out to see the world. I embarked on the greatest adventure of all: I got married and had children.

Over the years, I have taken great delight in doing outrageous things with my family, primarily to have fun but also, because I am a newspaper columnist, for something to write about. For example, in a vehicle marked with the words "Student Driver," I took the same road test Katie had to take when she was going for her driver's license. I called the White House to see if I could have Lauren's room declared a federal disaster area. I went to the bank to apply for a loan so I could buy Sue the $10-million Millennium Bra from Victoria's Secret. After reading that dogs not only have extensive vocabularies but that several of them participated in a blackjack tournament in Atlantic City, I played cards with our pooch, Lizzie – and lost.

These and dozens of other stories are in this book. They are all true. The names have not been changed to protect the innocent.

Over the years, I also have learned many things. Here are some of them:

* Children not only don't want to be seen with their parents, they don't want other people to know they even have them.

* Kids don't understand the word "no" when you say it to them, but they know exactly what it means when they say it to you.

* Love your children without question. This will give you the patience to put up with all their questions.

* Fatherhood is why beer was invented.

* Children are priceless, but they cost a fortune.

* Families are not democracies.

* The point at which children begin to realize that Dad isn't as smart as they thought is when they ask him for help with their algebra homework.

* A lot of parents say they don't want to be a burden to their children. Not me. Being a burden is my goal. And if you ask my children, I achieved it long ago.

* The telephone is an instrument of communication that has done more to ruin communication between parents and their children than any device ever invented.

* Men don't know where anything is. Women do – except if a man asks. Then it's never there.

* The surest sign of maturity in a man, if indeed it ever happens, is when he comes to appreciate Shemp.

* Milestones are like kidney stones: They're hard to pass, but at least after you pass a kidney stone, you feel better.

* The keys to a happy marriage: Love each other, honor each other, respect each other. And for God's sake, put the cap back on the toothpaste!

Now that I have reached middle age, that wonderful stage of life between changing your kids' diapers and needing them yourself, I have learned something else: Wisdom comes too late in life to be useful to you and is best passed on to your children, who aren't wise enough to realize that you finally know what you're talking about.

My children have both moved out, which means I am suffering from empty nest syndrome. When they were home, I suffered from empty head syndrome. In between, I learned life's most important lesson: Love conquers all. So, I might add, does laughter. Not long ago, during a reflective moment in the quiet of our empty nest, Sue said to me, "We've never had much money, but we've always had a lot of fun."

That's what our lives – and this book – are about.

CHAPTER 1:
"CHILDREN OF A LESSER DAD"

"Why Kids Are Hard of Hearing"

My children won't listen to me. I don't take this personally because they won't listen to my wife, either. Their annoying refusal to pay attention to anything we say is symptomatic of a malady that strikes all children during the difficult years between infancy and whenever they move out of the house.

This is why the average child has to be told something nine times before he or she will even bat an eyelash. Unfortunately, it means that if you have two children, you have to repeat yourself 18 times. If you have three kids, 27 times. And so on.

The all-time record in our house is 148 times. It was set one night last week when Sue and I told Katie and Lauren, who are 9 and 7 years old, to get ready for bed.

"All right," I said, switching off the TV, which they had been watching through eyes that had more glaze than a Christmas ham, "it's time to brush your teeth and hit the sack."

No response.

"Come on," Sue chimed in. "You've got school tomorrow."

Still nothing.

"Do you girls think we're talking to the wall?" I asked in a tone of growing annoyance.

One of them started to play with the cat.

"LEAVE THAT POOR ANIMAL ALONE AND GET UPSTAIRS!" I screamed.

"Okaaaaaaaaaay," they whined in unison, finally acknowledging our urgent pleas but, in doing so, sounding remarkably like fingernails scraping across a blackboard.

This does not mean, however, that they went straight upstairs. No, sir. They fiddled and fussed with this and that before making their way to the bathroom, where more cajolery was needed to make them stop fooling around and get to bed. By that time, Sue and I were so exhausted that *we* had to call it a night.

The problem, of course, is that this sort of thing happens all the time. And not just in our house. I know people who have practically had to be institutionalized after trying to get their kids to do their homework. Even getting your kids to do something they *like* requires persistence beyond the bounds of nature.

Why? I have two theories. One is that most children, for reasons unexplained by science, are struck temporarily deaf at inopportune moments. How else do you account for their utter lack of responsiveness when you say something to them? Why they are never struck deaf when they are talking to their friends, or watching their favorite TV shows, or listening to the hottest musical group is, of course, an even greater mystery.

That is why I put more stock in my second theory, which holds that something in children's brains (a proton, a neutron, a moron) automatically scrambles or, more likely, mutes any message delivered in the voice of one of their parents. Let's say you want your daughter to clean her room. You articulate this very clearly, but when the sound of your voice penetrates your child's ear, it registers either as a numbing buzz or as something that sounds an awful lot like, "Don't get up. I'll do it." The response is usually a vacant stare or, if you are lucky, an incomprehensible mumble, followed by a continuation of whatever she was doing.

How should parents deal with this kind of exasperating inaction? Some believe in administering a mild form of corporal punishment, which is fine if your child happens to be a corporal. Others opt for a suspension of certain privileges, such as food and water.

I suggest a more subtle technique. The next time your kids ask you for something, pretend you have been struck deaf. You may also give them a vacant stare or, if you are feeling particularly playful, an incomprehensible mumble. Then go back to whatever you were doing. They'll soon get the message.

Of course, nothing can replace open and honest communication between parents and their children. As a matter of fact, I had a heartfelt talk with my daughters about this very thing a couple of nights ago, just before they were supposed to go to bed.

Unfortunately, they didn't listen to a word I said.

"Parents Shouldn't Be Seen or Heard"

I am an embarrassment to my children. So, for that matter, is my wife.

This hardly comes as a surprise because, as invariably happens in households headed by two pathetically out-of-touch old fogies, the kids have reached an age where it is decidedly uncool not only to be seen with your parents, but even to have them.

That became sadly obvious when Katie, who is 11, asked us to bring her to the local skating rink for something called Rock Night, a rather loud and crowded affair in which all the "def" kids in town get together so they can "dis" their relatives and join their "rad" friends in looking "dope" while falling on their "keisters" out on the ice.

Apparently this popular weekly event is called Rock Night because the kids expect their parents to crawl under a rock and stay there until the whole thing is over.

At least that is what I thought we were supposed to do after Katie announced, in loving and considerate tones, that unless she needed money to buy something at the snack bar, she didn't even want to be seen with us.

At this point I told her, in a moving display of fatherly devotion, that I was going to drive home and come back in 15 minutes with a huge sign saying: "I AM KATIE ZEZIMA'S FATHER!"

A look of utter panic swept over my daughter's face. "Noooooo!" she shrieked, and ran off frantically to join her pals at the ticket window.

"We're certainly lucky to be held in such high esteem," Sue said as we stood inconspicuously in a corner with a motley group of other parental outcasts.

"Indeed we are," I said gratefully. "And to show our appreciation, let's take the money we've been saving for her college education and blow it in Atlantic City!"

Lauren, meanwhile, is at the age (9) where any public display of affection, especially when it is committed on school grounds, is treated as if you had an advanced case of leprosy.

The usual reaction in this situation is a look of absolute terror, followed by either a stern warning, uttered through clenched teeth, of "Dad! Stop it!" or a quick turn of the head, as if to say to anyone who might be watching, "I don't know this clown."

I would be remiss if I did not admit that members of my generation reacted pretty much the same way whenever our parents had the audacity to be seen on the same continent with us.

The greatest potential for disaster was being dropped off at school in the morning, not just because you were considered a dweeb if you didn't take the bus, but because your mom, on rainy or snowy days, would invariably call your name as you slithered away from the car like a gangster heading for the federal courthouse and, in a voice loud enough for everyone to hear, cheerfully shout, "Don't forget your rubbers!"

Today, of course, the phrase "Don't forget your rubbers!" has an entirely different connotation. But that is beside the point. The point, as any cool and worldly young person will tell you, is: PARENTS ARE HUMILIATING VERMIN.

By now you are probably taking two aspirin and asking yourself: How can I avoid being an embarrassment to my children without spending thousands of dollars to send them to summer camp in Tibet?

Fortunately, there are several easy steps you can take. The first is to make yourself invisible. I recall that in the original version of "The Invisible Man," Claude Rains found the secret of invisibility in a drug called monocaine, which is supposedly derived from a plant that grows halfway around the world. Making the long trip to obtain this plant would be a small price to pay to spare your children the pain of being seen with you.

Another step you can take is to join the Federal Witness Protection Program. This would be a great relief to your kids because if they found themselves in an uncomfortable social situation, they could always identify you as someone else.

But perhaps the easiest step you can take if you must go out in public with your children is to be as inconspicuous as possible. Just stand in a corner with all the other embarrassingly uncool parents and look the other way.

And don't forget your rubbers.

"Going for Broke With Fundraisers"

Out of the goodness of my heart, not to mention my wallet, I am going to make all of you nice, kind, generous people out there an offer you can't (I hope) refuse:

How would you like to buy something from the fundraisers my kids recently brought home from school?

I hate to resort to such desperate measures, but at this point I will do anything to help the girls sell candy, wrapping paper, magazines and other items that nobody really needs so Sue and I won't have to buy $450 worth of the stuff ourselves.

That's the amount of merchandise Lauren has to sell for her school fundraiser in order to win one of the following valuable prizes: Laser Pinball (item 45A in the Super Prize Award Program), the Tonka Hyper Drivers Race Set (45B), Sportcraft Quadhockey (45C), the Tasco Telescope (45D), the Panasonic FM/AM Stereo Cassette Recorder (45E), Electronic Hot Shot Basketball by Milton Bradley (45F) or the GE Clock Radio Telephone (45G).

Lauren, who is in fifth grade, is leaning toward either the pinball game or the telephone, even though she is, at the moment, $358.50 short of her goal.

All is not lost, however, because if she sells $300 worth of merchandise, she can win one of 13 fabulous prizes, including Electronic Arcade Bowling (30D), the Two-Person Boat Set (30G) or the Bubble Tank Aquarium (30H).

Of course, she could always settle for a more modest prize (the Glitter Spinner, 21C, or the Southbend Spincast Fishing Outfit, 15B) if she sells merchandise totaling either $210 or $150.

The good news is that she has already qualified for the $90 prize package, which includes the Sportcraft Safety Dart Game (09C), the Giant Wall Watch (09F) and a game appropriately called Skip-It (09E).

Sue and I want her to win the Grand Prize, which is awarded for "The Highest Sale in School." This would enable us to select one of the following:

(a) Panasonic 19-inch Color Remote-Control Television

(b) Panasonic VCR

(c) Marriott Fun Family Weekend

Katie, who is in seventh grade, has been selling magazines for her fundraiser, which may already be over. I lost track. I am reasonably sure, however, that I am now a subscriber to Seventeen, Disney Adventures and a couple of other periodicals I don't really want.

If Sue and I have to contribute to even one more fundraiser (and there are more coming up), we won't be able to send our kids to college.

This is where you come in. Now listen carefully, because I, a person who ordinarily would be unable to sell snow shovels in Alaska, am going to launch into a sales pitch that would make P.T. Barnum proud.

Here it is: BUY SOMETHING!

Maybe you'd like the Musical Carolers, a hand-painted porcelain figurine featuring four Dickensian family carolers singing "Joy to the World." Price: $20.

Too expensive? Try the Holly Berry Candles ($5). Or the Merry Christmas Bicycle Bear ($4). Or the Microwave Splatter Shield (a steal at only $2).

How about the Kitten & Puppy Magnets ($3). Or All-Occasion Gift Wrap ($5). We're even selling Delicious Assorted Chocolates ($5).

While you are considering these fantastic bargains, let me say honestly that school fundraisers are held for a very good cause: to bankrupt every parent in the United States, as well as relatives, neighbors and co-workers who are invariably coerced into buying stuff, often from more than one child.

This is why some people, fearing they will have to sell their cars if asked to contribute to yet another fundraiser, have resorted to playing dead when approached by any child who isn't their own.

Still, I'm sure you would love Florentine Stationery ($8). Or the Photo Frame Carousel House ($6). Or the Shark Ice Scraper ($4).

It really doesn't matter, just as long as we sell enough merchandise to win the Marriott Fun Family Weekend. At this point, a free vacation is the only kind we can afford.

"In Softball, Girls Will Be Girls"

This Little League Update is brought to you by the Tooher-Ferraris Insurance Group, proud sponsor of the Tooher-Ferraris Fighting Adjusters, the girls' softball team I attempt to manage.

The good news for all you Tooher-Ferraris fans (and you know who you are) is that after opening the season with three consecutive defeats, we finally won our first game the other day. It was a huge upset, a wildly controversial 10-9 decision that was immediately appealed by the opposing manager, whose team, the Ronnie's Best Little Hair House Fighting Stylists, had been listed as heavy favorites by the oddsmakers in Las Vegas.

Despite the controversy, which was sparked by a last-inning collision at first base and required diplomatic intervention by the United Nations, the victory was just what we needed to turn this club around (the reason we lost our first three games, I now realize, is that we were facing the wrong way).

We have made great strides since preseason, when the team not only didn't have a sponsor, but some of the girls didn't even have gloves. (One of the fundamental rules of organized softball for girls 8 to 12 years of age is that just before every game, at least one player must show up and announce that she forgot her glove. According to a rarely invoked clause in the Little League Rule Book, if this fails to happen, the manager must select one girl to go back home and leave her glove there.)

Anyway, for the past three years, our sponsor had been a pediatric center called, oddly enough, the Pediatric Center, making us the Fighting Pediatricians.

Even though we enjoyed great success last season (my first as manager, during which we set the all-time team record for victories: three in 12 games), we found ourselves without sponsorship this spring.

For a while it looked as if we would be sponsored by Pudgie's Famous Chicken, a popular fast-food place. But the deal fell through about a week before Opening Day, which was probably just as well because we would have ended up being the Pudgie's Famous Fighting Chickens. This possibility, which wouldn't have fazed a boys' team, greatly upset the girls, who trembled at the thought of wearing fashionably incorrect uniforms emblazoned with the logo of a plucked hen.

(Speaking of uniforms, style is extremely important in girls' softball. Last year, for example, we had snazzy blue uniforms with white trim; this year we got stuck with bright yellow outfits with black lettering. As one of the outfielders astutely pointed out, "We look like a bunch of bananas!")

Nonetheless, it came as quite a relief when the father of two of our players, an insurance executive, generously offered to sponsor the team. In gratitude, I have faithfully complied with the Official Little League Managers' Guide, which states, in Article XXVII, Section 12, Aisle 6, Boston 4, Cleveland 0: "If you have a brain in your head, you will make sure the sponsor's kids get plenty of playing time."

The Guide also states that you should give your own kids (in this case, Katie and Lauren) enough playing time to avoid problems at home but not so much that parents of the other players will attempt to have you kicked out of the league for nepotism.

Another important duty for the manager of a girls' softball team is to hold the players' jewelry during games. This usually means stuffing your pockets with an assortment of rings, necklaces, bracelets, earrings, barrettes and, sometimes, pins, which can lead to a painful stint on the disabled list.

But probably the most satisfying job a manager has, one that requires a deft combination of patience and wisdom, is teaching the girls the fundamentals of the game, the two most important being:

(1) stop gabbing about snobbish classmates, cute boys, dumb parents, broken fingernails, etc., and PAY ATTENTION OUT THERE! and (2) don't play catch in the dugout.

This second rule was broken last week, when someone conked Lauren on the head and raised a welt roughly the size, ironically, of a softball. The only recourse a manager has in a situation like this is to seriously consider making the girl who threw the ball the starting pitcher.

Still, I am happy to report that the team is finally starting to jell and that we are ready for our next game, a key showdown with the Crescent Cleaners Fighting Steam Pressers. I just hope the girls remember to bring their gloves.

"Deliver Me From This Paper Route"

As a loving and devoted father, not to mention a man with absolutely no backbone, I would do anything for my children that did not involve algebra.

This may explain why I am now delivering newspapers.

I made the big career switch last Sunday morning, when Lauren, a young tycoon who has more money on her at any given moment than Sue and I have in our checking account, was snoozing peacefully at a friend's house.

This created something of a problem because Lauren is, as you already may have guessed, a papergirl. Or, to be politically correct, a "paper carrier," which is, I suppose, better than being a typhoid carrier.

At any rate, it dawned on Lauren, just before she left on Saturday afternoon, that she wouldn't be around the next morning to deliver her papers.

"Don't worry," Sue said reassuringly, taking the burden off the child and selflessly placing it on her own shoulders. "Your father will do it."

This was a classic example of the motherly instinct to protect her offspring at all costs, even going so far as to volunteer the services of the hapless man who, as is so often the case, had no choice in the matter.

"So it has come to this," I said to no one in particular, because no one in particular would listen to me. "Almost 20 years in journalism. Now I have a paper route."

It was pretty discouraging considering I went into this field for what I think are two very noble reasons: I wouldn't have to get up early and I wouldn't have to do any heavy lifting.

Imagine my dismay when I found out I would have to get out of bed at a time when vampires are getting in so I could lug the newsprint equivalent of a refrigerator around the neighborhood.

That's because this was the Sunday paper, which has to be delivered early so subscribers can sit around in their underwear and complain about all the bad news over coffee and doughnuts.

Also, each Sunday paper contains so many sections, inserts and promotional giveaways (one of these days it's going to come with radial tires) that a man in my condition could easily rupture a vital organ just trying to find the sports section.

As I began my route, which Lauren had mapped out for me on a piece of paper that looked like the battle plans for the invasion of Normandy, I had three major concerns:

1. I would have a heart attack.
2. I would deliver papers to the wrong people.
3. I would be recognized by the neighbors.

Fortunately, the first two things did not happen. I did, however, suffer an anxiety attack when I realized that, with 21 customers, I would have to make three trips. As I limped along with those unbearably bulky newspapers stuffed into a huge, heavy bag, the strap of which was cutting off the blood supply to my neck, I must have looked like Quasimodo. I had a hunch that would happen.

It made me wonder: How does Lauren do it? I guess it's because she is 28 years younger than I am. She's also an athlete who is in excellent shape. Then again, some dead people are in better shape than I am.

But the worst part was listening to the wisecracks of the neighbors I encountered on my route.

"Did you get a promotion?" one of them asked.

"You're really moving up in the world!" another one said with a snicker. Even his dog seemed amused.

At least it wasn't raining. And at least I didn't have to collect money from all those people in their underwear, some of whom, I was sure, would come to the door in their nightgowns, with curlers in their hair and beauty cream on their faces, and they'd grumble as they handed over $1.50 or whatever they owed, and I would be forced to smile blandly and say, "Thank you, Mr. Smith."

When it was all over, I stumbled inside and, like the trouper that I am, went back to bed.

That's why I have great respect for all those dedicated young paper carriers who get up early and go out in all kinds of weather to deliver papers so that people who care deeply about what is going on in the world can read drivel like this.

The next time Lauren sleeps over a friend's house, I'll probably be your paperboy again. It wouldn't kill you to leave me a nice tip.

"The Yolk's on Him"

Noel Coward once said that only mad dogs and Englishmen go out in the midday sun. If Coward had been around during the recent heat wave instead of using the feeble excuse that he has been dead for the past 20 years, he might have added newspaper columnists – or at least me – to the list.

That's because I bravely (not to mention stupidly) ventured out into the midday sun last week to find out, in the interests of science, as well as home economics, if it is possible to fry eggs on asphalt.

The result: three runny eggs, sunny side up, and one fried brain, over easy.

The motivation for my gourmet experiment, as I will gladly explain to the Nobel Prize committee once I regain all my faculties, was simple: I didn't have anything better to do.

Neither, apparently, did Katie, who inspired me by conducting similar research in the driveway a couple of days earlier, with mixed – or, rather, scrambled – results.

For the sake of accuracy, it must be noted that the scrambling was purely accidental, occurring when the eggs were run over by a car. This greatly reduced their nutritional value.

That is why I took Katie along for my landmark study, which I conducted in a nearby school parking lot that I knew would be empty. I also brought Lauren, as well as my nephew, Jordan, and my niece, Vicki, all of whom acted with childlike enthusiasm and, against their better judgment, as my assistants.

Sue, clearly the only sensible one of the bunch and a woman who says she does enough cooking, thank you, decided to stay home in air-conditioned comfort. Wimp.

I knew that thousands of people try to fry eggs on sidewalks or in parking lots or on the roofs of cars every summer. So, just to be different, which only served to prove that the heat was really getting to me, I attempted to cook an entire breakfast.

In addition to three eggs, which I wrapped in napkins and gently placed in a Tupperware container, I packed a couple of strips of bacon. Too bad we didn't have any hash browns.

My cooking equipment included a frying pan, a spatula, a tub of butter and a roll of paper towels.

At precisely 1:10 p.m., as the sun blazed high in the sky, I piled the kids into the car and drove over to the parking lot for what surely would be the scientific discovery of the century. Or at least the week.

And the conditions were perfect. The temperature that afternoon hit 98 degrees. Unfortunately, our outside thermometer broke last winter and I couldn't find the family thermometer (oral, by the way), which I wanted to use to measure the temperature of the asphalt.

Nonetheless, as soon as I stepped out of the car, I estimated that the ground temperature was high enough to kill a camel.

As the children looked on excitedly, I cracked the first egg on the asphalt. Nothing happened. It just sat there, looking gooey.

Then I tried to fry another egg, plus the bacon, in the frying pan. My theory, which even the kids thought was stupid, was that the pan, being metal, would become so hot in the sun that the food would fry easily. No such luck. The egg ran and the bacon became soggy.

"This isn't working, Uncle Jerry," Vicki said.

"Patience," I said with an avuncular chuckle as I removed the last egg from the container. Then, with the precision of a professional chef, or at least a cook at McDonald's, I cracked it over the trunk of my brand-new car, which was scorching hot.

Unfortunately, at that exact moment, a cloud moved overhead, covering the sun and temporarily messing up an already failed experiment.

A few minutes later, the sun peeked out again, heating things up once more, though not nearly enough to help me make scientific or even culinary history. So I gave up, suffering from heat prostration and convinced that it would take two months of 98-degree weather to cook a two-minute egg.

Still, the one I had cracked on the asphalt, now lightly seasoned with bits of gravel, was at least beginning to congeal. I offered to take it home and finish cooking it for lunch.

For some reason, no one was interested. Must have been the cholesterol.

"How to Carve a Pumpkin"

One of the most cherished of Halloween traditions – aside from the time-honored prank of leaving a flaming bag of dog poop on your neighbor's front porch, ringing his doorbell, and then hiding in the bushes so you can watch his reaction when he tries to stamp it out – is the carving of the pumpkin.

This is a rewarding and wonderfully relaxing ritual that not only brings the family closer together, but entails the use of sharp and potentially dangerous implements that invariably leads to bloodshed.

In order to carve a pumpkin, you must first drive to a pumpkin farm to buy one. Although pumpkins may be purchased at nearby grocery stores, they are usually too puny or lopsided to satisfy the children, meaning you must get in the car on a Sunday afternoon when a good football game is on TV and motor halfway across the state to pick out a pumpkin suitable for carving.

(Note: Federal law requires the nearest pumpkin farm to be no closer to your house than 50 miles, thus ensuring that you get the recommended annual viewing of fall foliage all in one day.)

Once at the farm, you can usually choose from literally hundreds of pumpkins – none of which the kiddies can agree upon. Their incessant squabbling results in the slow ebbing of parental patience, finally prompting you to snarl, "If you don't STOP right this MINUTE, we're going home WITHOUT a pumpkin!"

As you make this idle threat, someone walks by and looks at you with a wary eye, as if to say, "What's the matter, pal? Too much caffeine?"

After settling on a pumpkin that turns out to be the size of Dr. Ruth Westheimer, you must stand in line with it for half an hour, then lug it all the way back to the car, which you have parked in the next county because approximately 100,000 people decided to buy their pumpkins on the very same day.

This part of the ritual complete, you can now move on to Phase II, which entails leaving the pumpkin on the front porch until: (a) some neighborhood punks come along and smash it all over your driveway or (b) it rots.

The proper way to deal with either situation is to sit with your head in your hands and moan, "I am NOT going back to the pumpkin farm. So help me, I am NOT going back. You can't make me. ..." Blackberry brandy can help, too.

At long last, it is Halloween – time to carve your pumpkin. To do the job right, you will need:

1. A gas mask
2. A chain saw
3. A tourniquet
4. A transfusion
5. A priest

I am only kidding about No. 5. But you should know that this little exercise isn't quite as easy as some people would have you believe.

The first thing you should do is place the pumpkin on the table and get the chain saw. Since your spouse is not likely to let you use it in the house (except, perhaps, to slice meatloaf), you will have to opt for a steak knife.

Hold the stem of the pumpkin firmly in one hand and the knife firmly in the other. Then try to cut a circle around the stem (so you can make a lid) without either breaking the blade or slicing your thumb off.

You will notice that the top doesn't come off easily. That's because it is attached to the disgusting pulpy mass inside the pumpkin. When you dig this stuff out, it smells bad enough to curl the wallpaper.

Once you have scooped out the seeds (a trowel works just fine), you should place them on a piece of newspaper, which must then fall to the floor so the seeds may become permanently embedded in the carpeting.

Now comes the really fun part: carving the face. As you struggle to make the traditional triangle eyes and pointy-toothed smile, you should be keenly aware that fingers, wrists and major arteries are more vulnerable to stab wounds than first imagined.

After you have finished your masterpiece, you should put it back on the front porch, take off the lid and place a candle inside. This not only creates an eerie night glow, but it helps show off the blood stains.

The best part is that once Halloween is over, you don't have to wait for some neighborhood punks to come along and smash your pumpkin. You can go outside and do it yourself.

CHAPTER 2:
"TEENGLISH SPOKEN HERE"

"You Don't Say"

In my children's eyes, which have cost me a small fortune in optometric care, I am pathetically ill-informed about today's youth. I would feel tremendous guilt about this except for one thing: Today's kids know even less about what is going on in their lives than I do.

I base this belief on the following conversation, which takes place in thousands of American homes every day:

Parent: "How was school today?"

Child: "Fine."

Parent: "What did you do?"

Child: "Nothing."

Parent: "Do you have any homework?"

Child: "I don't know."

Ask your child about any subject directly involving him or her and you will get one of three responses: (a) "Fine," (b) "Nothing" or (c) "I don't know."

If your child is in a particularly talkative mood, and by some miracle is not on the phone, you'll get all three. Otherwise, your mere existence will be deemed too annoying to acknowledge, in which case your child will pretend not to hear you.

Besides, kids are always listening to mind-numbingly awful music played at decibel levels high enough to blow out the windows, so your child may not be ignoring you. He or she may simply be deaf.

Still, it's alarming to know that even though everything is "fine," absolutely "nothing" happens in school. Why? "I don't know." I do know, however, that when our kids are the leaders of this country, we may hear this:

Reporter: "Mr. President, how did the summit go today?"

President: "Fine."

Reporter: "What did you discuss?"

President: "Nothing."

Reporter: "Does this mean the world is on the brink of nuclear disaster?"

President: "I don't know."

How can our kids have no idea what is going on in their lives? In recent weeks, I have asked my daughters the following simple questions: What time does your field hockey game start? When is the parade you're marching in? Am I supposed to pick you up at church after religious instructions? Who's driving you home from school? How are you? Who are you?

Each time, the response has been: "I don't know."

When I was a kid, things were different. When my parents asked me how school was, I would always say, "Great!" When they asked what I did in school, I would respond, "Stuff." When they asked if I had any homework, I would answer, "No."

I lied, of course, but at least I lied creatively. And I always made it sound as if I were actually doing something, worthless though it often was. I never said, "I don't know."

Another irritating response today's parents get is: "Nobody." For example, if the phone rings and your child answers it and stays on the line for 45 minutes and eventually, because of a house fire or something, has to hang up, and you ask who called, the response you will almost always get is: "Nobody."

And the really scary part is that your child's friend will say the same thing to his or her parents when they ask the same question. Maybe that's why some people grow up to be nobodies.

All I can say, parents, is that if you want to find out what is going on in your children's lives and you expect to get more than three words out of them, call them on the telephone.

"Language Barrier"

Now that Katie and Lauren are teenagers, they have become fluent in a mysterious language called Teenglish. For American parents, Teenglish is a lot like Chinese, only more confusing.

It's also like English in that it contains actual English words. But instead of being spoken clearly and intelligibly, these words are blurted out like machine-gun fire, with a few mumbles thrown in just to ensure that adult listeners will think they are suffering from a rare neurological disorder.

Following are two examples that illustrate the differences between English and Teenglish.

Example No. 1:

Teenager (in approximate English): "I hate to tell you this, but I, like, got suspended from school today for, ya know, hitting my, like, algebra teacher in the nose with a spitball."

Parent: "Good shot!"

Example No. 2:

Teenager (in Teenglish): "IhatetotellyouthisbutIlikegotsuspended-mumblemumblemumblenosewithaspitball."

Parent: "What?"

This can be rather unsettling. When Katie started to speak Teenglish around the house, I had no idea she had learned an entirely new language. Instead, I thought there was something wrong with me. "Am I going deaf or is Katie impossible to understand?" I would ask Sue. To which she would reply, "What?"

Things got really bad when one of Katie's friends, a very sweet and personable girl, started leaving messages like this on the answering machine: "HiKatiethisisJenit's4o'clockI'mjustcallingmumblemumblemumblecallmewhenyougetbackbye!"

At one point I considered going to a specialist to see if I needed treatment that would result in the following spectacular headlines:

Doctors Remove 47-Pound Ball
Of Earwax From Head
Of Confused Father
Patient: 'I can hear again!'

Fortunately, such a radical procedure was unnecessary. I know so because other parents have told me that they can't understand their teenage children, either. This raises two interesting questions:

1. Was I like this when I was a teenager? (Answer: I'm too old to remember.)

2. How the heck can these kids understand each other?

First teen: "Ithinkmyfather'sdeafeverytimeIsaysomethingmumble mumblemumblehe'shopeless."

Second teen (nodding): "Liketellmeaboutityaknowmumblemum-blemumblehahaha!"

But the worst part is that they actually get mad at you when you can't figure out what they're saying. This always happens after you stare blankly at them and say, "What?" They will then shake their heads and reply, "Never mind."

"Driving Yourself Crazy"

Not many parents know this, mainly because they spend most of their time in the car, but on the same day that Henry Ford manufactured the first automobile, his wife asked him a very important question: "Could you pick up the kids at school this afternoon?"

From that day on, Ford and his wife couldn't leave the house without driving their children somewhere.

Today, Sue and I, like millions of American parents, find ourselves in the same situation: We have become full-time (and unpaid) chauffeurs for our kids.

This is the greatest of all parental responsibilities. Feeding and clothing your children are not nearly as important as driving them all over town every day, sometimes to so many different places that you could become a millionaire in just one week if only you had the nerve to install a meter in the family car. Of course, you'd never collect. You will find, much to your dismay, that your kids are even cheaper than you are, although they usually have more cash, almost all of which is yours anyway. And even if you did collect, you'd have to spend the money on gas.

At this moment, the family car has 36,926 miles on it. I would conservatively estimate that Sue and I have put 35,248 miles on it while driving Katie and Lauren – and sometimes their friends – to and from various destinations and important engagements.

These include: school, the mall, the library, the skating rink, friends' houses, fast-food joints, piano lessons, school dances, school plays, school concerts, field hockey practice, field hockey games, basketball practice, basketball games, softball practice, softball games, soccer practice, soccer games, band practice, football games, drama club, tutoring programs, religious instructions, the movies, the video store, the variety store and the school supply store. Then we drive home, only to turn right around and go out again.

It's a wonder the car doesn't explode.

A lot of people think I am only 3 feet tall because the only time they see me is when I am sitting in the car. (These same people, incidentally, think Sue is 1-foot-10.)

Of course, Sue and I are not in this alone. We are one small part of a vast network of parents and grandparents whose main mission in life is to provide transportation for children who often show their appreciation either by fighting in the back seat or by switching the car radio from your station, which plays good stuff like oldies or classic rock, to some god-awful station that plays what your parents, when you did this to them, always called "garbage."

A space launch is probably easier to plan than a typical day of chauffeuring. Here is a chilling example.

Sue: "Can you pick up Lauren at school today? She gets out at 2:30."

Me: "I guess so. But doesn't she have drama club?"

Sue: "That's Wednesday. Today's Thursday."

Me: "Oh."

Sue: "Drop her off at home. My father is bringing Katie to her tutoring program. I'll bring her home after that."

Me: "Who?"

Sue: "Katie."

Me (confused): "I thought she was going to the mall."

Sue: "I brought her and Traci there yesterday. Traci's mother drove them back."

Me (more confused): "What about Lauren's basketball practice?"

Sue: "She goes to basketball Wednesdays at 5:30. After that I have to pick her up and drop her off at religious instructions at 6:30. You pick her up at 7:45, remember?"

Me: "Yeah."

Sue: "Katie has band tonight at 6. Katalin's mother is bringing her. Can you pick them up at 8 and drive Katalin home?"

Me: "I thought Katie had band on Tuesdays."

Sue: "She does."

Me (totally confused): "But you said today's Thursday."

Sue: "It is. She has band tonight, too. They have to play at the football game tomorrow night."

Me: "That's Friday."

Sue: "No kidding. It's also the night you have to pick up Lauren and Farha at the rink. Farha's mother is driving them over there."

Me: "Good."

Sue: "Any questions?"

Me: "Just one. What day is this again?"

"The Pajama Game"

Because I have a fashion plate in my head, I have always believed that if you are going to sleep on the job, you might as well dress for it. That is why I recently wore pajamas to work.

I decided to leave the house looking like I had just rolled out of bed because Katie and Lauren, who think I am the most uncool man in America, have joined all their cool friends in wearing pajamas to school.

I noticed this disturbing trend one morning when Lauren, who is 13, came downstairs and announced that she was going to school. I saw that she was wearing hiking boots, a sweatshirt, an outer jacket and – much to my astonishment – a pair of plaid flannel pajama bottoms.

"Aren't you going to get ready for school?" I asked.

"I *am* ready," Lauren replied.

"You're not dressed."

"Yes, I am."

"You're wearing pajamas!"

"Dad," Lauren said, rolling her eyes, "it's the new style." Then she kissed me on my obviously empty head and went to school. About 10 minutes later, Katie, who is 15, left for school dressed the same way.

"What the hell is going on?" I asked Sue.

"Where have you been?" she wanted to know. "This is what the kids are wearing."

That's when the idea hit me: If the girls think I am so uncool, I'll prove them wrong. So I decided, for one day and one day only, to wear pajamas to work.

The next morning, after Katie and Lauren had gone to school, I came downstairs wearing shoes, a shirt, an outer jacket and – much to Sue's astonishment – a pair of plaid flannel pajama bottoms. Because I'm a professional, I also wore a tie.

"I'm glad I'm not going to be seen with you," Sue said. But that did not stop her from sending me out on some errands before I went to work.

My first stop was the bank, where I got in line with about half a dozen people. Nobody wanted to make eye contact with me. I could tell what they were thinking: "My God, he's got a gun."

When I got to the window, Lisa, the teller, took one look at me and asked, "Are you going to work like that?"

"Yes," I replied.

She was stunned. Then she made a suggestion: "Why don't you withdraw some money, go to the store and buy yourself a pair of pants?"

I didn't have time because I had to go to the post office, where I got in another line. Again, no one wanted to acknowledge me, but it wasn't hard to discern everybody's worst fear: For once, a customer would go postal.

At the window, where I bought a book of stamps, Hubert, the clerk, smiled and said, "I'm going to have a pajama party and you're the first guy I'm going to invite."

"Thanks!" I said. Then I went to work.

Al, the security guard, asked, "Is that the new style?"

"It sure is," I responded.

He shook his head and said, "I wouldn't wear it."

Upstairs, I was the hit of the newsroom. One woman thought I was wearing golf pants. I don't play golf. Another woman, the fashion editor, said I was very stylish. A third woman winked at me and said, "You look cute."

I sat down and didn't get up for the rest of the day. At the end of my shift, I went home, where my daughters were giddy with excitement.

"You're a virtual fashion slave!" Katie exclaimed.

Lauren beamed at me and said, "Dad, you're so cool."

It was the ultimate compliment. I'll probably never hear it again.

"Road Test"

According to statistics that must be true or I wouldn't have made them up, four out of five teenagers are better drivers than their parents. The fifth teen, unfortunately, is the maniac responsible for the outrageous cost of everyone else's auto insurance.

This sad fact was recently driven home (in an old Chevy Cavalier with the words "Student Driver" on the bumper) after the occurrence of two unnerving events:

1. Katie got her driver's license.
2. I took a student driving test.

It all began the day I drove Katie, who had just turned 16, to the Lewis School of Driving in New Canaan, Connecticut, so she could take her written test, her vision test and, of course, her driving test.

After an hour or so, I got tired of waiting around, so I went upstairs. I poked my empty skull into an equally empty classroom — the kids were out on the road by this time — and encountered an avuncular gentleman named Hagen Morris, also known as Inspector No. 107 of the Connecticut Department of Motor Vehicles. Having nothing better to do, I asked, "Would you mind if I took the written test?"

Inspector Morris, a jolly old elf who laughed when he saw me in spite of himself, replied, "Why not?"

So I sat down, took out a pen and breezed through the 16 multiple-choice questions. Having been sworn to secrecy, I cannot reveal what they were, but I can tell you this: I got four wrong. One more and I would have flunked.

"Your daughter did better than you," said Inspector Morris, adding insult to injury by noting that she got all 16 right.

Then I asked if I could take the eye test. Naturally, I had left my glasses, which I wear only for driving, in the car. The vast majority of the time, I can't find my glasses. Once, as I was about to go out on a cold winter's day, I ran around the house like a madman, my car keys in my right hand, my gloves in my left, screaming that I couldn't find my glasses. My wife and both of my daughters stared at me, slack-jawed, in utter disbelief. Even the dog seemed incredulous. Finally, my wife, trying futilely to suppress a cackle, pointed and said, "They're in your hand!"

Sure enough, there they were, along with my gloves, in my left hand. It was then that I came up with a brilliant idea: prescription windshields.

I decided not to go downstairs to get my glasses, so I took the vision test without them. I placed my eyes against the lenses of the boxy gray screening machine, which beckoned with the promise of a bizarre peep show, and indeed beheld strange figures. They were, I was told, letters of the alphabet. One of them (I think it was a Q) looked like the chemical symbol for boron. So much for thrills. I was pronounced legally blind.

When I asked if I could take a driving test, Inspector Morris chuckled and said, "I flunk my wife every time we go out. She doesn't want to drive anymore."

Then he said I would have to set it up with Sgt. Richard Istvan of the state DMV, a very nice guy who kindly arranged for my humiliation.

Five days later (and one day after Katie got her license), I went to Tom's Driving School in Greenwich, Connecticut, to take my road test with Ralph Cafiero, Inspector No. 40, an affable gent who nonetheless was extremely serious about his job.

"I hope you realize," said Inspector Cafiero, "that if you fail, I can take your license away."

I gulped. Then I got into the "Student Driver" vehicle with the dutiful inspector, who had a clipboard. I buckled up, checked the mirrors, turned on the signal and, after putting on my glasses, which were in my left hand, eased out of the parking lot. As a matter of pride, I was determined to do well.

In a span of about 10 minutes, I had committed three major infractions.

My first mistake came at a busy intersection. As I approached, the traffic light turned from green (which means "go") to yellow (which means either "apply brakes" or "floor it!"). I did neither. I was in the traffic twilight zone, being neither far enough from the light to stop comfortably nor close enough to it to slip past legally. If I had jammed on the brakes, two things would have happened:

1. The car would have come to a screeching halt in the middle of the intersection, where it probably would have been broadsided by a vehicle racing through from the opposite direction.

2. Inspector Cafiero would have been thrown forward with such violence that the air bag would have deployed and driven his clipboard directly into one of his nostrils.

So I casually cruised past the light just as it was turning red. Inspector Cafiero made a menacing black check mark on the official test form attached to his clipboard.

After he instructed me to turn off the main road and onto a side street, I approached another intersection. This one had a stop sign. The thing to do in this situation, Katie often told me when she was taking her driver's education class, is to pull up to the white line in front of the stop sign, come to halt and count "one one-thousand, two one-thousand, three one-thousand." Then you are supposed to inch up to the stop sign itself and come to another halt, after which you should look both ways before slowly and carefully proceeding.

In real life, however, the guy behind you would have got out of his car while you were on "two one-thousand" and smashed your windshield with a baseball bat.

I had this in mind as I approached the stop sign. Nobody else was coming from any direction. I glided up to the sign and came to what is popularly known as a "rolling stop," although I did look both ways before slowly and carefully proceeding. Inspector Cafiero made another black check mark on his clipboard.

My third infraction was for speeding, if by "speeding" you mean going faster than a tortoise with a broken leg. During the road test I watched the speedometer diligently, never going above the speed limit. On one brief stretch, however, the speed limit was 25. As anyone who has ever been behind the wheel of a car will tell you, doing 25 is like being parked. Inspector Cafiero looked over at the speedometer.

I looked down at it. I was doing 30. Yet another black check mark appeared.

"You can't pass this test," said Inspector Cafiero.

And I didn't. I flunked.

"If it's any consolation," I was told, "most adults have fallen into so many bad driving habits that they couldn't pass, either."

At least I didn't have an accident.

Afterward, Inspector Cafiero kindly said I could keep my license but suggested that I brush up on my driving skills.

"Get a good driver to give you some pointers," he said. Then he smiled and added: "Why don't you ask your daughter?"

"Brain Drain"

As a man whose two daughters made it through their teenage years without, miraculously, forcing me to file for bankruptcy, I have often said that when your children selfishly insist on eating every day, money comes in handy.

Now I know why. According to a story in the Journal of Neuroscience, there is a significant difference in the developing teenage brain and the mature brain of an adult when faced with the opportunity to make money.

Scientists found that as adults worked to make money in a research task, they experienced an increase in blood flow in the nucleus accumbens, a region deep in the middle of the brain. In contrast, adolescents between the ages of 12 and 17 who performed the same research task had half the blood flow and volume in this region.

"It tells us that teenagers love stuff but aren't as willing to get off the couch to get it as adults are," said James Bjork, one of the scientists who conducted the study.

I don't want to disparage the scientists or minimize their research, but any parent who has ever had a teenager could have told them that. Besides, I don't think this study gives teens enough credit for having the brainpower to obtain the money they need for the stuff they love.

In fact, I'll go even further and say that it's the teenagers who are enterprising and the adults who are lazy.

Using my own research, which was conducted at home during Katie and Lauren's teenage years, I can say unequivocally that the increased blood flow in the nucleus accumbens region of the adult brain occurs as the result of constant demands by teenagers for money, leading to a common medical condition in parents known as high blood pressure.

This has a profound effect on the thought processes of parents, who are eventually rendered helpless, and therefore lazy, in the face of such relentless assaults. The following typical conversation serves as an example.

Mother (standing in the kitchen): "Your daughter wanted 50 bucks yesterday to get her hair cut."

Father: "My daughter? She's yours, too. Maybe that's why she hit me up for 30 bucks so she could go to the mall."

Mother: "You're too easy."

Father: "Me? You're the one who got her into the shopping habit."

Mother: "It's about time we put our feet down."

Father: "You're right. This kid must think we're made of money."

Mother: "From now on, we have to learn how to say no."

Teenager (yelling from the couch): "I need a new backpack to carry my books in or I'm gonna flunk out of school."

Mother (rushing into the family room): "Sure, honey."

Father (taking out his wallet): "How much do you need?"

In fairness to teens, they can't get jobs until they turn 16, which is why I tried for so many years, starting when my kids were in elementary school, to get the child labor laws repealed. Now it's too late. Besides, even if teenagers do get jobs, they need transportation, which means you have to buy them a car or they have to use yours. Either way, with gas and insurance costs, you're out even more money.

Eventually, teenagers get off the couch so they can go places to spend the money their parents have given to them. The parents, in turn, get older and more tired from working so hard to make the money their teenagers need. This is why parents spend an increasing amount of time on the couch, where they usually fall asleep and miss not only the 11 o'clock news but also their teenagers, who come in late and can't get up in the morning and spend a large portion of their precious little time at home on the couch, thus leading parents to believe, wrongly, that teenagers are lazy.

I guess those scientists don't have kids.

And now, to the parents of teenagers, I will report the final and most important part of my research: If you think your money supply is low and your blood pressure is high now, just wait until they go to college.

CHAPTER 3:
"COLLEGE DAZE"

"What I Learned on My College Tour"

Ever since Sue and I got back from taking Katie on her first college tour, many other parents with children in high school and not enough money in the bank have asked for my expert advice on how to prepare for such a trip.

Now that the shock has finally worn off, and the swelling in my feet has gone down, I am happy to oblige. In return, I ask only that you make a small contribution to the Jerry's Kids College and Hideous Wardrobe Fund. All donations are tax deductible.

On our three-day trip to the Boston area, we saw four schools: Holy Cross, Boston College, Boston University and Tufts. This was an exciting and extremely educational experience that taught me three valuable lessons:

1. Wear comfortable shoes.
2. Bring plenty of aspirin.
3. Keep your mouth shut.

The first lesson came five minutes into our tour of Holy Cross, an excellent institution of higher learning. In fact, the learning couldn't get much higher because the school is situated on the side of a mountain and must have been built by the Sierra Club.

Comfortable shoes – sneakers, docksiders, maybe bedroom slippers – are absolutely necessary for a tour of any college campus, even a small one and even one on level ground, and even then your feet will swell to the size of watermelons.

You should start planning your tour months in advance by joining a health club. Remember, you are old and pathetically out of shape. You don't want to strain your heart while schlepping all over campus. Save the cardiac problems for when you are sitting in the information session or, if you can arrange it, your personal interview with a representative from the admissions office.

This is where I learned the second lesson: You must pretend to be interested in academics, housing, cultural life, etc., while waiting for an opportunity to casually inquire what the hell all this is going to cost and if, please God, you might qualify for financial aid. After hearing the terrible truth, you should pop a fistful of aspirin. If that doesn't work, you might want to go back to your hotel and take some stronger medicine, such as Scotch.

The final lesson I learned on our college tour is this: Don't embarrass your son or daughter by making stupid remarks. Your mere existence, even if you don't say anything, is likely to be humiliating to your children, no matter what their age.

Naturally, during our trip I said too many dumb things to remember. The low point came on a walking tour of Boston University. As we passed a science building, Nicole, one of our student tour guides, said something about the study of voltronics. "Does anybody know what voltronics is?" she asked.

So everybody could hear, I shouted: "Weren't they a Motown group?" Katie didn't look at me for the rest of the tour.

For now it's over, but I am sure there are more college tours to come. We will probably head south soon to see, among other schools, William & Mary. Right now, unfortunately, we can only afford Mary.

"Disaster Area"

Parents, does your child's room look like a cyclone hit it? Is there so much stuff on the floor that you're afraid the place will be condemned by the board of health? Is the room so messy that you wouldn't be surprised if the remains of Jimmy Hoffa were in there?

Here's some helpful advice: Call the White House to ask if your child's room can be declared a disaster area. Then you'd be eligible for federal funds to clean it up.

That's what I did after Lauren came home from college for the summer.

I must say that Lauren is a wonderful young woman. She's smart, funny, independent, considerate and beautiful. In other words, everything I wasn't when I was her age. Or even now.

But she's not exactly the neatest person in the world. The shocking thing is that her room at college looked like something out of Good Housekeeping. It was so clean it could have passed the white glove test.

Unfortunately, her room at home couldn't pass the toxic glove test.

An elephant carcass and the fuselage of Amelia Earhart's plane could be in there and you'd never know it because they'd be buried under a mountain of laundry. An inventory, which I took one day from the door because I couldn't get into the room without breaking my neck, revealed the following: three large plastic boxes, two suitcases, two shopping bags, a duffel bag and one big cardboard box, all filled with clothes that had spilled onto the floor. Scattered over the floor itself were approximately 150 articles of clothing, not to mention cosmetics, hair care products, CDs, videos, a computer, a bowl of popcorn, half a glass of soda, an unmade bed and lots of other items I either couldn't identify or am afraid to think about.

I have heard many parents describe their children's rooms as disaster areas. So I thought: Why not see if Lauren's room qualifies?

First I called the governor's office and was transferred to Dennis Michalski, director of community affairs for the New York State Emergency Management Office.

"Funny thing you should call about this," Michalski said. "I picked up my son at college last week and by the next day he had already revamped his room."

"Is it a disaster area?" I asked.

"Last time I looked, yes," Michalski admitted.

"I'm hoping the governor will declare my daughter's room a disaster area so I can get state funding to clean it up," I said.

"There is no disaster fund in New York State for this kind of thing," Michalski explained. "If there is a disaster in your house, it stays in your house. In this case, you are stuck with the disaster in your daughter's room. We can only try to bring you back to pre-disaster conditions."

"Could the state send over some heavy equipment to get all that stuff out?" I asked.

"We could notify the police or the highway department," Michalski said. "We'd use all the assets of the state, with response personnel and trucks, but if the disaster exceeds our capability – and in this case it sounds like it would – the next step is to ask for federal assistance."

I thanked Michalski, wished him luck with his son's room and called the White House. Although his track record in this area hasn't been too good, it was clearly a job for President George W. Bush, who, like me, has two daughters, Jenna and Barbara, who are about the same ages as Katie and Lauren. I wanted to know not only if the president would declare Lauren's room a disaster area, which would qualify me for federal funds, but if he had ever declared his daughters' rooms disaster areas.

"That would be classified information," said Noelia Rodriguez, press secretary for first lady Laura Bush, to whom I was transferred after being told by someone in the press office that the president was too busy to take my call.

"Does Mrs. Bush think Jenna and Barbara's rooms are messy?" I asked Rodriguez.

"I can't talk about that," she said. "I wouldn't even go there."

"My wife has given up on Lauren's room," I told her.

No word yet from the president, who has his own messes to deal with. But as Rodriguez suggested, we may have to wait until Lauren goes back to school in the fall to get her room cleaned up.

"In the meantime," Rodriguez said helpfully, "you might want to keep the door closed."

"Final Exam"

As a proud father, I am happy to say that Katie recently graduated from college with a BA in history. As a pinched parent, I am relieved to say that I recently graduated from college with a BS in economics. This degree was unofficially conferred upon me, money cum laude, because over the past four years I have learned a valuable lesson: College economics is a lot of BS.

The final exam came in the mail exactly a week before Katie was to graduate from a prestigious institution of higher learning. To protect its privacy, I will identify it only as a university in Boston whose mascot is a dog, which is what parents have to work like to afford to send their children there.

The exam, a take-home test that was addressed to Katie but was sent to Sue and me, because colleges know that students have even less money than their parents, involved advanced mathematics. The last question, based on a yearly tuition of $35,000, which otherwise would be frittered away on such luxuries as food and shelter, was as follows: "A reminder: Your student account balance must be resolved in order that any diploma(s), transcript(s) and/or other certifications of academic records may be issued. Please send your payment now to assure that your balance is resolved. Amount due: $4,635.00."

The test wasn't multiple choice. It was no choice. Pay up or your kid doesn't graduate. I looked at the bottom of the page, expecting to see the signature of Vito Corleone.

This made me consider bank robbery. But parents of college students should dismiss this idea, as I did four years ago, because no bank in the United States has enough money in its vault to pay for your child's college education.

That is why I think the federal government should adopt what I call the Reverse Education Plan. It is based on the long-held scientific belief that a person's greatest capacity for learning is when he or she is a toddler.

My proposal: Send children to college first. That way, they could get a university degree right off the bat. Then they could work their way down through the educational system until, in their final year, they would go to kindergarten, where they could play "Simon Says" and learn how to get along with others just prior to becoming legal adults.

Under this system, parents wouldn't have to wait 18 years for the cost of a college education to skyrocket to the point where it rivaled the gross national product of Finland. True, they wouldn't have time to save, either. Then again, if you lived to be 100, which at this rate is extremely unlikely, you couldn't save that much money.

Here's my advice: Don't even bother saving for college. This contradicts everything the experts say. But the experts can afford to send their children to college because they are paid a lot of money to tell other people to save enough money to pay for college. Don't believe them. It can't be done.

What can parents do to prepare for this financial challenge? They should, on a daily or even hourly basis, impart to their children these gentle words of wisdom: "Get off the phone!"

From the time they start elementary school until the day they graduate from high school, the vast majority of kids, boys as well as girls, spend approximately 98 percent of their nonschool waking hours gabbing on the telephone. Parents should tell them, even if it means calling them up, that they would be better off spending their time studying, because if they don't study they will never get into college and will have to settle for low-paying, dead-end jobs that entail asking other people if they want French fries.

If this shameless ploy works well enough, your children will qualify for scholarships and you will receive financial aid, which means that the budding scholars will actually be admitted to college before you have to start paying for it. The downside is that if you die before the loans are paid off, there are heavy penalties, so it pays to stay alive. See your doctor. If he says the strain of paying for college is too much on your heart, get a second opinion. But don't expect your HMO to cover it.

Along the way, you will periodically receive little surprises such as the one Sue and I got the week before Katie was supposed to graduate. Fortunately, it all worked out (we owned only $1,000, so the mortgage was late) and we were able to attend the graduation ceremony without being accompanied by sheriffs.

Even though I didn't get a diploma, I know my economics degree will come in handy: Lauren still has two years of college to go.

"The New Roommate"

With apologies to John Steinbeck, whose wrath I don't have to worry about, I am thinking of writing a book titled "Of Mice and Men

With Daughters in College Who Expect Their Fathers to Drive All the Way to School to Exterminate the Mice in Their Rooms."

It should be required reading, not only for all college students, but for their fathers, who can use it to get a degree in either psychology or pest control. Granted, no parent needs another tuition bill, but when you're already paying for an off-campus apartment that your daughter won't stay in because she saw a mouse, you can't help but fall into the trap. If only the mouse would do the same, you wouldn't have this trouble.

The crisis began about a week and a half ago when I got this message from Lauren on my answering machine: "Hi. It's me. It's 3 o'clock. Please call me back when you get this. It's very, very important. I found a mouse in my room and I'm very disturbed. So please call me back. Goodbye."

My immediate thought was: "She's more than two hours away. What does she expect me to do about this?"

To find out, I called her back. In a quavering voice, Lauren described her hair-raising (for both her and the mouse, I'm sure) encounter: "I was lying in bed when I saw this thing run across the room. It was a mouse. A baby mouse."

"A baby mouse?"

"Yes. It was really small."

"They're the worst kind. Remember the time one of your gerbils got loose and we couldn't find it? I thought it was going to climb into my bed in the middle of the night and chew my face off."

"Dad! Stop it! This is a serious matter."

So serious, in fact, that Lauren had "evidence" of an invasion: She saw scratch marks on a box of Girl Scout cookies and had to throw it out. Worse, she had to do the same with a box of Godiva chocolates.

"Maybe the mouse has a sweet tooth," I told her, wondering to myself why I was shelling out bundles of money for tuition when she already had enough of her own money to buy Godiva chocolates.

Then I asked if she had called the school's buildings and grounds department. "Yes," Lauren reported angrily. "They sent over this old guy who laughed at me."

It was undoubtedly because she was dressed to kill. As she described it, her mouse-hunting outfit consisted of a T-shirt, boxer shorts, leather shoes belonging to her boyfriend and a pair of rubber gloves with which she wielded a broom in one hand and a can of Lysol in the other.

"I'm surprised you didn't scare the mouse to death," I said.

"The mouse isn't dead," Lauren said. "I don't know where it is. Now I'm going to have to clean my room and spend a hundred dollars to wash my clothes." Then she added: "I'm not sleeping in there."

The next day, I called Lauren for an update and was told that she had bought three mousetraps and put peanut butter in each one but that the mouse hadn't been caught.

In one of the daily briefings that followed, Lauren reported that the mouse was "trying to outsmart me" because the peanut butter was slowly disappearing. She also said that she had, indeed, cleaned her room. "I never thought it would come to that," she said sadly. "Do you know how paranoid I am?"

I had an inkling when Lauren said she was sleeping on a couch in another room. She also said that her boyfriend had a mouse in his room last year. It kept eating cheese from the traps he had set but was never caught. "It didn't bother him," Lauren said. "Guys don't care."

That gave me an idea: Besides me, the only other male in our house is Henry, one of our four cats, who routinely exterminates little critters in our yard. "I can send him up there to dispatch the mouse," I told Lauren.

"Don't send him up over the weekend," she replied. "We're having a party."

As of this writing, the mouse hasn't been caught. But if it's captured alive, I am going to bring it home and put it under Lauren's bed. If that doesn't make her keep her room clean over the summer, nothing will.

"A Moving Experience"

If I have learned anything in the past six years, during which I have had one or both of my daughters in college, it is this: If the tuition bills won't give you a heart attack, moving your kids into and out of their dorm rooms will.

That is why I am lucky I have lived long enough to say, with a severe shortness of breath and quite a bit of chest pain, that I have just moved Lauren out of college for the last time.

For a parent, this is the equivalent of winning a gold medal in the Olympics. In fact, college moving should be an Olympic sport. ("The judges have all given Jerry Zezima perfect scores of 6.0 for lugging that massive suitcase from the car all the way up to his daughter's room. Unfortunately, he has collapsed at the finish line.")

Or it could be – and I am claiming intellectual property here, which means I want a percentage of the profits – a TV reality show. I can see it now: "Survivor: College Moving Day." Sponsored by Allstate insurance ("Because Daddy won't be here forever") and Bayer aspirin ("Doctors recommend it. Do not use if already dead").

As I said to Sue the first time we took Katie to college: "By the time both kids are out, we should have this down to a science." I may have flunked science in college, but I was absolutely right about moving.

The mistake parents make when their children are freshmen is overdoing it. Before Katie went to school, Sue took her shopping and bought enough stuff to clothe, feed and pamper quintuplets. (Imagine five kids in college!) Then we rented a vehicle the size of a condominium to accommodate everything.

By the time Lauren was in college, we used our own cars – mine, Sue's and, after she got her driver's license, Lauren's. Sometimes, it still wasn't enough.

Over the years, Sue and I learned and strictly obeyed the following Rules of College Moving.

Rule No. 1: Choose a parking space that is actually closer to your house than it is to your child's dormitory or apartment building.

Rule No. 2: Choose an elevator that is not working. After waiting for half an hour, you must fight other parents to cram into the building's only working elevator, which is required by federal law to smell like a can of sardines. This odor must emanate, specifically, from you.

Rule No. 3: If you are a father, you must lug the heaviest stuff up to your child's room, dump it there and go back for more. After you have brought everything up, you should seek medical attention while your wife makes the bed, decorates the room and puts everything where she thinks it should go. After you leave, your child will rearrange the room and put everything where it really should go – on the floor.

Rule No. 4: If it is the end of the school year, see Rule No. 3 and do the opposite.

Rule No. 5: Drive back home. This trip should be made in silence. The only communication between spouses should involve cursing.

In six years, Sue and I made 16 trips to and from college, eight for each daughter. In the two overlapping years when they both were in school, we made eight trips, four each year. One year, I had to take Katie to school on the same day Sue took Lauren. The father of one of Lauren's roommates kindly helped Sue lug Lauren's stuff up to her room after he had moved his own daughter in. I think he has since passed away. I, of course, had to move Katie in myself. I couldn't feed myself for three days.

On Mother's Day, Sue and I moved Lauren out for the last time. As I was lugging one of her massive suitcases out to the car, which at least was parked close to her building, I passed another father who was going back up to his daughter's room. "This is it," he said, wiping the sweat from his brow. "She's a senior. Thank God."

I nodded knowingly and said, "We survived."

Now all that's left is to pay off those tuition bills. I don't know if my heart can take it.

CHAPTER 4:
"PET PROJECTS"

"Taste Test Is the Cat's Meow"

According to a sophisticated and highly scientific taste test conducted the other day in my kitchen, two out of three humans prefer Kal Kan cat food to other leading brands.

This came as a surprise – I thought a gourmet product like Fancy Feast would top the list – but when it comes to eating cat food, you can never be too finicky.

I was prompted to conduct the test after watching the recent appearance of professional pet food taster Edwin Rose on "Late Show With David Letterman." Rose, who comes from England, which is not exactly known for its human food, tried to explain to Dave what he does for a living. I expected some profound insight into the methods Rose uses to rate pet food, how he got into this highly respected but rather lonely profession, which brands taste best, what kinds are most nutritious, etc., but the man let me down.

Not only did Rose end up consuming less pet food than Dave, who was wolfing the stuff down like he hadn't eaten in a week, but this so-called "expert" didn't even talk about cat products, sticking instead to dog food.

As the proud owner of Ramona, the world's dumbest cat, who finally showed a shred of intelligence by refusing to participate in my taste test, I was disappointed.

So was Katie, a 14-year-old Letterman fan who suggested that I conduct my own research. But when I asked if she wanted to take part in this landmark study, she immediately said her busy social schedule wouldn't permit it.

Still, I did manage to assemble a distinguished panel of judges: Lauren, who is 11; my niece, Vicki, who is 8; and yours truly, who is old enough to know better.

Our sole aim, in addition to grossing each other out, was to help you, the consumer, determine which canned cat food is best for your kitty.

We decided to test nine brands (one for each life we expected to lose as a result of eating the stuff). The brands were: Friskies (sliced chicken with gravy), 9 Lives (sliced beef in gravy), Whiskas (mealtime), Sheba (poultry liver with aspic), Alpo Premium (tuna treat), Fancy Feast Gourmet Cat Food (sliced turkey feast), Stop & Shop (chopped grill dinner), Purina (hearty stew) and Kal Kan Optimum (with chicken and rice).

The first thing we noticed was that all the brands, no matter what flavor, contained the following three ingredients: meat byproducts, poultry byproducts and water sufficient for processing. We ate them anyway.

Vicki and I rated Friskies, the first item on the menu, as OK. Lauren said, "It makes me want to throw up in the beginning, but the aftertaste is good."

Both Lauren and Vicki spat out 9 Lives (I thought it was pretty tasty), but all three of us liked Whiskas, which, aside from a rather grainy consistency and the fact that I found a piece of rubber in it, tickled the palate.

Sheba was pretty bland (don't come back, little Sheba) and Alpo got mixed reviews. I liked it. Vicki said, "It's tuna! I HATE tuna!" Lauren said, "Eeeewwww!"

Fancy Feast, which is hawked in those annoyingly precious TV commercials by that noted feline epicure Lauren Bacall, fared somewhat better. Vicki said, "That's good! I like that one!" Lauren (my daughter, not Bacall) also liked it but preferred Whiskas. Ditto for me.

Stop & Shop, which contained bits of what I thought was gravel, was not high on our list.

Vicki summed up our feelings about Purina when she said, "I like my mom's cooking better than this."

As it turned out, we saved the best for last. As far as Lauren and I were concerned, Kal Kan was the kat's meow. "Mmmm! I like this one!" said Lauren, savoring the soft grains of rice and hearty chunks of chicken. I liked it so much that I had a second helping.

Only Vicki didn't rate Kal Kan as the best brand, ranking it a notch below Fancy Feast.

For dessert, we each had a Pounce tartar control crunchy cat treat ("Because cats can't brush").

So there you have it, cat lovers. Edwin Rose couldn't have done any better. Maybe Dave will want to have us on his show.

But just the thought of all those leftovers, which Sue has threatened to serve for dinner, makes me want to cough up a hairball.

"Love Connection"

WARNING: The following column is rated PG (for "procreating gerbils"). It contains mature subject matter. It also contains matter that is pretty immature. Parents are strongly cautioned: If there are parts you don't understand, just ask your kids.

Joseph and Star gazed longingly into each other's beady red eyes.

"Squeak, squeak," Joseph said, nuzzling Star's seductively furry form.

"Peep, peep," Star responded eagerly, submitting to an urge she could no longer control.

They embraced and fell into a pile of cedar chips. Afterward, they shared a tiny cigarette.

All right, so gerbils don't smoke. But they do all that other stuff. I know this because Sue and I are the Masters and Johnson of the gerbil world.

We're also, I guess, grandparents.

This sordid tale of love and lust began last month when Lauren, who is 12, brought home a houseguest. His name was Joseph.

The idea was to introduce Joseph, a weaselly studmuffin who lives in Lauren's seventh-grade classroom, to Star, a mousy female who resides in our basement. The result, Lauren hoped, would be a litter of adorable little baby gerbils.

Of course, this was just an excuse for an immature innocent to watch shocking acts of animal passion. I sort of enjoyed it.

Not that I am overly fond of gerbils, which are essentially rats with decent haircuts. Lauren's friend Holly has 12 of them. In my opinion, that's a dozen more than any family should have.

We once had a gerbil named Melanie, an annoying little beast who kept trying to break out of her cage by ramming the top with her head. I assume she gave herself a concussion because the next day, tragically, she was dead. Lauren was devastated. I had a beer. After a moment of silence, we buried Melanie in a solemn Dumpsterside service.

A few days later, we got another gerbil (I forget the name) who also died under mysterious circumstances.

Now we have Star. At least she hasn't killed herself yet.

For my money, hamsters are far superior. Not only are they cute and friendly, but they are pretty laid back. If they're not eating pellets or playing in their wheels, they're sleeping. Gerbils, on the other hand, are always jumping around like they're wired on caffeine. They also like to stare at you menacingly with their bloodshot eyes, as if to say: "I'm gonna bust outta here tonight and bite your nose off when you're sleeping." It's a bit unnerving.

But that didn't stop Lauren from bringing Joseph home during spring vacation. Naturally, Joseph and Star hit it off right away. First he bought her a drink (there's a water bottle in Star's cage). Then he whispered sweet nothings into her pointy ear.

You can imagine what happened next. Then imagine it happening for an entire week. I get tired just thinking about it.

When school resumed, Joseph went back. Now he's an absentee father. Last week, after much drama and speculation, Star gave birth to six of the ugliest little creatures you have ever seen. They look like raisins with feet.

Even though two didn't make it (they probably died from fright after seeing me), we are all proud of the other four, which Star, to her credit, has not eaten.

To eliminate the controversy in sex education, I think the public schools should tell their students to get gerbils and take notes. I also think bums like Joseph should pay child support.

"Doggie Dentistry"

My dog has bad breath. This wouldn't be a problem if she brushed her teeth, but either she can't reach the toothpaste or she just doesn't care. So, on orders from her doctor, who almost fainted when he checked out her canines during a recent office visit, I have to brush them for her.

This is the ultimate indignity for a dog owner. Standing in the rain, or the snow, or the dark of night, holding one end of a leash and pretending not to notice what is going on while your best friend is taking care of business at the other end, and then having to engineer sanitation in full view of gawking pedestrians and passing motorists, is nothing compared to brushing your dog's teeth.

My career in doggie dentistry began the day Sue and I took our beloved mutt, Lizzie, to the vet for a checkup. This included a series of shots (to guard against everything except, alas, halitosis), a prescription (for heartworm pills, which I ought to take myself), a diagnosis ("She's too fat") and a bill, which came to more than $200, not one penny of which was covered under our HMO (Healthy Mongrel Organization).

The vet also checked Lizzie's pearly yellows, his eyes blinking violently in reaction to the toxic fumes that emanated from her mouth, and announced that she had plaque. "Someone has to brush her teeth," he said, coughing slightly.

"Who?" I asked.

The vet looked at me. Sue looked at me. Lizzie looked at me.

"I guess you're elected," the vet told me. Then he said, "This is very important for your dog's health."

Really? What about my health? Wasn't the vet almost asphyxiated when he opened Lizzie's mouth? Couldn't bacteria from her gums invade my bloodstream and turn me into a raving lunatic who barks at the mailman and chases squirrels? And what if I died? Would I get a dignified funeral ("He was struck down in the prime of life by canine gingivitis") or would Lizzie dig a hole and bury me in the backyard?

"You don't want her to get sick, do you?" the vet asked.

"Of course not," Sue piped up.

So it was settled. I would be in charge of brushing the dog's teeth. But first I had to learn how. I received a crash course from a veterinary assistant named Kristen, who explained that the process is slow but "very pleasurable and rewarding."

"For whom?" I wanted to know.

"For both of you!" Kristen chirped.

Then she handed me the C.E.T. Fingerbrush Kit, which contained a fingerbrush (a soft rubber toothbrush that looks like a thimble with short bristles on one side) and a tube of poultry-flavored "enzymatic dentrifice" (doggie toothpaste). On the back of the kit were instructions on how to brush your dog's teeth.

"You'll have a beautiful smile, won't you, Lizzie?" said Kristen.

"Woof!" said Lizzie.

"Ruff!" I replied, and closed the door.

Lizzie is a cherished member of our family. She is sweet, smart and slobbering. If a burglar broke into our house, she would either drown him in kisses or help him carry out all our valuables.

Therein lay the challenge of brushing her teeth: Lizzie is a pooch who loves to smooch. It was doubtful I could get anywhere near her kisser without being kissed. But I had to try.

The night after our visit to the doctor, I opened Lizzie's mouth and examined her teeth. The vet was right: Her breath was strong enough to choke a horse. It was like being at a bean supper with the windows closed.

I quickly clamped Lizzie's mouth shut and started to read the back of the doggie dental kit. It began: "Caring for your pet's teeth is as important as caring for your own." Suddenly it hit me: Maybe I should start eating dog biscuits.

Then I read Step 1: "Find a quiet, convenient time when you and your pet are both relaxed." This was impossible. Whenever Lizzie sees me, she wants to play. We routinely chase each other around the house, play hide and seek, have a catch with her toys, bark at each other and otherwise create such a disturbance that I am surprised the neighbors haven't called the police. Still, to make sure at least one of us was relaxed, I had a glass of wine.

Step 2 said: "Acquaint your pet with the process. For the first few days, simply hold your pet as you normally do when petting him or her. Gently stroke the outside of your pet's cheeks with your finger." I did this for a few minutes at a time for the first few days. Instead of laying on the kisses, Lizzie regarded me warily out of the corner of her eye, as if to say, "He's up to something."

Step 2 continued: "After your pet becomes comfortable with this activity, place a small dab of the dentrifice on your finger and let him or her sample it. Pets usually like the taste of dentrifice and consider it a treat."

Sure enough, Lizzie lapped it up. And why not? The stuff is supposed to be poultry-flavored, and Lizzie, who has a delicate stomach, is on a special diet consisting almost exclusively of chicken. One night, before giving her some of the dentrifice, I put my nose to the tube and took a whiff. I couldn't smell anything. Then again, I'm not a bloodhound. So I put a gob of dentrifice on my finger. I sniffed it. Nothing. So I figured, what the hell? I gulped the gob. It did not taste like chicken.

Step 3 said: "Introduce the fingerbrush. Slide it onto your index finger. Place a small amount of dentrifice on the brush. In a slow, circular motion, brush one tooth and the adjoining gumline. The purpose of this step is to get your pet accustomed to the feel of the brush."

I tried, but Lizzie licked the dentrifice off the fingerbrush before it had even touched a tooth. I tried again. Lizzie gave me her paw. I tried a third time. She started kissing me.

A week later, we were ready for Step 4: "Begin brushing. Over the next several days, gradually increase the number of teeth brushed. Go slowly and gently. Do not go beyond your pet's point of comfort."

By this time, I was well beyond mine. But I worked diligently, night after night, without surgical gloves or a gas mask, in a heroic display of unconditional love, to clean my dog's teeth and freshen her breath.

"Build up to approximately 30 seconds of brushing on each side," the instructions went on.

I am now up to eight seconds of brushing on each side. But it has been well worth the effort. Already Lizzie's breath is less offensive, and her smile can almost be described as beautiful. I only hope her teeth are white before I reach the age when my own begin to fall out.

"Mind Over Matter"

My dog is psychic. I always knew Lizzie was smart (she takes after Sue), but I didn't realize she had telepathic powers until I read a magazine article on Sonya Fitzpatrick, the star of TV's "Pet Psychic," who revealed her secrets for helping people tune in to their pets.

I like Sonya and enjoy her show, which I try to watch with Lizzie, if only so she can take comfort in the fact that she's not as nutty as some of the critters that Sonya psychoanalyzes. But most of the time Lizzie would rather play. The rest of the time she falls asleep. Maybe she's jealous.

When I read the article on Sonya in the current issue of Family Circle, and learned that you don't have to be Dr. Dolittle to talk with the animals, I thought I would try to communicate telepathically with Lizzie.

Lizzie and I have always been able to read each other's minds, which in my case is the equivalent of the introductory lesson in an Evelyn Wood course.

Lizzie's mind is a bit more complicated, but essentially our communication involves playing, eating, taking a ride in the C-A-R and going for a W-A-L-K. (I can never say these words out loud without setting Lizzie off in a frenzy of excitement. I am writing them this way because Lizzie is sitting next to me and might see the screen. I don't know what I am going to do when she learns to spell.)

At any rate, I was guided by Sonya's Secrets to Tuning in to Your Pet.

The first of her seven secrets was: "Begin with a calm and tranquil mind and seek out a calm atmosphere for you and your pet."

To ensure a calm and tranquil mind, I had a glass of wine. Lizzie, who is only 7 and therefore not of legal drinking age (though in dog years she is exactly as old as I am), had a bowl of water. I chose the living room for a calm atmosphere because Sue, who had already communicated to me that she thought I had gone over the edge, was watching TV in the family room.

I called Lizzie telepathically. Nothing happened. So I called her verbally. She sauntered into the living room holding in her mouth one of the six dozen toys in her collection. She wanted to P-L-A-Y.

Then I followed Secret No. 2: "Say your pet's name telepathically to get its attention." I did. Lizzie dropped her toy and stared at me. It was then that I realized she was communicating telepathically with me. She said, "What the heck are you doing?"

Secret No. 3: "Visualize your pet as you say its name." To do this, I closed my eyes. I could hear Lizzie walking away. I called her back telepathically. It didn't work. "Lizzie!" I shouted. She returned with the toy in her mouth.

Secret No. 4: "Send your pet a picture of its physical body along with its name." I imagined Lizzie's plump black and white body and sent it to her. I imagined her name and sent that to her, too. Here's what Lizzie sent back to me: "Daddy's crazy."

At this point, she was either too confused or too scared to move, so she plopped down on the floor. I plopped down next to her. She looked at me for a moment, then tried to avoid eye contact.

Secret No. 5: "Ask your pet if there is anything it would like to do, then imagine your pet is sending you an answer. Accept whatever you receive." I asked Lizzie, "What would you like to do?" Her answer: "I'd like to get the hell out of here!"

Secret No. 6: "Always acknowledge the answer you receive." I said to Lizzie, "I don't blame you." It seemed to calm her down.

Secret No. 7: "Continue to ask your pet questions and remember to trust whatever answers you receive." I asked Lizzie, "Do you want to play?" She jumped up, grabbed her toy and led me on a chase around the house.

All in all, the session went well. In fact, I may start my own TV show. Lizzie thinks I should call it "The Pet Psycho."

"A Ruff Game"

Because I am not playing with a full deck, I will never be a high roller in Atlantic City or Las Vegas. That was painfully obvious the other night when I lost a blackjack tournament to my dog.

This low-stakes showdown was prompted by two recent news stories about man's supposedly best friend.

In the first story, by The Associated Press, German researchers have found a border collie named Rico who understands more than 200 words and can learn new ones as quickly as many children.

Patti Strand, an American Kennel Club board member, called the report "good news for those of us who talk to our dogs." She added, "The researchers have proven that people who talk to their dogs are cutting-edge communicators, not just a bunch of eccentrics."

Referring to dogs, one of the researchers, Julia Fischer, said, "You don't have to be able to talk to understand a lot."

In the second story, also by AP, the Sands Casino Hotel in Atlantic City recently re-created artist C.M. Coolidge's famous painting "Dogs Playing Poker" by using five dogs to play in a blackjack tournament.

Unfortunately, they didn't play their hands (or, rather, their paws) well. Tiny Chip, a Great Swiss, had three cards totaling 19 but took another card anyway. He busted. So did Jack Attack, a Rottweiler whose favorite words are "Hit me." He was sitting pretty with 18 but still wanted another card. He got a 7 of diamonds and busted with 25. Lucky Louise, who like the German genius Rico is a border collie, cheated by sniffing the other dogs' cards.

When I read these two stories, I knew that my dog, Lizzie, not only could beat Rico in an IQ test, but could play cards better than those pooches in Atlantic City.

Lizzie is part border collie, part terrier and part Italian. She also is very smart, with a vocabulary much larger than 200 words, some of which, such as C-A-R and W-A-L-K, I have to spell out because otherwise she will go crazy. In fact, I talk to Lizzie all the time, which makes me a cutting-edge communicator and not, as is widely believed, an eccentric.

The other day I bought a deck of cards. That evening, Lizzie and I played blackjack. The rules, as I explained them to her, were these: The first one to win 10 games is the champion. Anything over 21 is a bust. And no cheating by sniffing the other player's cards.

As we sat on the floor in the living room (we don't have a card table), I shuffled the deck and asked Lizzie to cut the cards. She did so by using her paw to separate about a third of them from the rest of the deck.

Then I dealt Lizzie a jack and a 10. I dealt myself a jack and a 4. I said to Lizzie, "Hit?" She just looked at me. So I said, "Stay?" She gave me her paw. She knows the word "stay," of course, but I didn't realize she knew what it meant in blackjack. I told you she's smart. She stayed with 20. I had 14, so I took another card. It was a 10. I busted. Lizzie won the first game.

"Beginner's luck," I told her.

"Ruff," she replied.

Lizzie's luck continued, and at one point she was leading, 5 games to 2. But I caught up, then went ahead, 8-7, only to see Lizzie rally and tie the tournament at 9-9.

One more game for the title. There was a lot of nervous panting. Lizzie was panting, too. I dealt her an 8 and a 7. "Hit?" I asked. She gave me her paw. I dealt her a 2. I asked Lizzie if she wanted another hit, but she played it safe and didn't respond. "Stay?" I asked. She gave me her paw. She was holding at 17.

I had a 5 and a jack. I had to take a hit. It was another jack. I busted! Lizzie won! I had been defeated by a dog.

When it comes to blackjack, I'm an L-O-S-E-R. Just ask Lizzie.

"Open Door Policy"

As a man with one dog, four cats and an occasional family of fleas, I have adopted an open-door policy. That's because I am constantly opening the door so my pets can go in and out of the house, either singly, in pairs, in groups of three or four, or all together, approximately once every three seconds or 147 times a day, whichever is more.

I would wear a cap and a fancy uniform except that: (a) I probably couldn't get into the doormen's union and (b) animals are lousy tippers.

As it is, I pretty much have to stand guard, either by the door in the kitchen or by the one in the family room, letting this one in or that one out. Sometimes I get so confused that I let myself out and can't get back in because the door is locked and neither the dog nor any of the cats has a key or can even reach the doorknob.

So I have to scratch at the door until Sue opens it and lets me in. Then I say "woof" or "meow," depending on my mood, and wait for a treat.

The players in this daily drama are Lizzie, the world's kissingest dog; Ramona, the world's stupidest cat; a kitty who, because nobody could think of a name for her, now answers to Kitty; and Kitty's kitties: Bernice, the party girl of Long Island, New York, and Henry, the only other male in the house.

The supporting players are two pairs of French doors that we recently had installed. The gang seems to have taken a special interest in them because they actually open and close instead of sliding like our old glass doors, which I guess were not as much fun.

I wasn't keen on French doors because Lizzie is not a French poodle (she's an American mutt) and I don't speak French, although I know enough to ask the dog, when she is barking at the door, "Do you have to go oui oui?"

Sometimes this is her No. 1 priority, but other times she just wants to sit outside because either there is a rerun on Animal Planet or the weather is nice and she wants to work on her tan. So she stands by the door and barks. I let her out.

Exactly 10 seconds later, Kitty wants to go out. I open the door. Kitty goes out and Henry, who went out five minutes earlier, comes in.

I sit down. Seven seconds later, Bernice wants to go out. I get up and open the door. Bernice goes out and Kitty comes in.

I close the door and sit down again. I hear barking. "Lizzie wants to come in," Sue says. I get up and let Lizzie in. Two minutes later, there is scratching at the door. It's Bernice, who wants to come in. I get up and let her in. As I open the door, Henry goes out again.

Ramona, who generally stays inside, sits by the door. If it's a nice day, she'll go out for a few minutes and come right back in. When this happens, the other three cats come in or go out, depending on where they were originally or if they think it would annoy Daddy.

Often, when one of them wants to go out, I will open the door and the cat will just stand there, undecided about what to do. "Make up your mind!" I cry. The cat will turn around and run into the next room. Fifteen seconds later, another one will want to go out. When I let that one out, the first one goes out, too. As soon as I go back to what I was doing, the dog will want to go out.

It goes on like this all day and well into the evening. I won't even get into what happens when I sit down to dinner. I haven't had a hot meal in three years.

If I didn't love my pets, I'd show them all the door. But why bother? A minute later, I'd have to get up to let them in again.

"Lizzie Meets Lassie"

Every dog has its day. For my dog, Lizzie, that day came a couple of weeks ago when I took her to the W Hotel in New York City to meet Lassie.

It was a once-in-a-lifetime opportunity to see a genuine superstar, a very special canine who not only has achieved fame for her talent and heroics, but is beloved by children and adults across the globe. I could tell Lassie was thrilled. And a little bit awed.

After all, Lizzie did win the blue ribbon last year in the Pooch Who Can Smooch competition at Puttin' on the Dog, the annual talent show and Adopt-A-Dog fundraiser, which is held in Greenwich, Connecticut, and regularly draws about 5,000 people, many celebrity judges and several hundred canine contestants. Lizzie also has been the star of numerous columns that have appeared in newspapers across the country and around the world. She has even been on the public radio show "Marketplace." But she has never let fame go to her pretty head and has remained sweet and unaffected.

Lassie has done all right for herself, too. She is a Hollywood icon whose latest movie is "Lassie" (the producers chose the title so people wouldn't mistake her for Lizzie, I guess). She's even an entrepreneur with a new line of pet food, biscuits and treats called Lassie Natural Way.

When Lizzie and I walked into Suite 1805 at the W, which must have stood for Woof, Lassie was sitting on a couch, surrounded by her entourage, including her trainer, Carol Riggins; her veterinarian, Dr. Jeffrey Werber; and her agent, John Fraser.

Lizzie and Lassie hit it off right away, greeting each other with kisses on both cheeks, Hollywood style. It was nice to see that these two major stars wouldn't be getting into a cat fight.

Lizzie, true to her standing as Pooch Who Can Smooch champion, was air-kissing everyone in the room. "You might want to trademark Lizzie's air kisses," said Fraser, adding that he'd be honored to be her agent, too.

I must confess that I was hoping Lizzie would land a movie deal (her first film would be, of course, "Lizzie"). I also could envision writing her Academy Award acceptance speech: "Arf, arf, arf!" (Translation: "You like me, you really like me!")

But then reality set in. "Lizzie's beautiful, but she's a little too pleasantly plump," Werber said diplomatically. "In order for her to look good walking down the red carpet, she'd have to lose a few pounds."

Naturally, he recommended that Lizzie change her diet and start eating Lassie Natural Way products, which are available in supermarkets nationwide. They seem to have helped Lassie keep her girlish figure.

But when Riggins offered Lizzie a treat, she politely declined. Maybe her feelings were hurt. To show Lizzie how good the treats are, I ate one. Actually, it wasn't bad. I only wish I had a beer to wash it down with, but I was told that Lassie just drinks water.

Riggins put a treat on Lassie's nose. On command, Lassie flipped the treat into the air and snapped it up. What talent! Then I tried it. Riggins put a treat on my nose. On command, I flipped it into the air, but it bounced off my mustache and fell to the floor. "You need more practice," Riggins said.

As all this was going on, scenes from Lassie's new movie, which got a special screening at the Tribeca Film Festival, were playing on a screen behind us. Lassie wasn't even watching. "She's already seen it," Fraser explained. I asked if Lassie ever got tired of saving Timmy on the old TV show. "The stupid kid was always falling down a well or getting trapped in a cave and Lassie would have to run for help," I noted. "She played those scenes with great enthusiasm."

"Lassie is a good actor," Fraser said.

I asked about persistent rumors that Lassie isn't really a girl. "I told you she's a good actor," Fraser replied with a wink.

She's also very sweet. And, like Lizzie, unaffected by her fame and talent.

After we all posed for pictures, and Lassie gave Lizzie a pawtograph, it was time to leave. The two stars said goodbye with one last air kiss. Then Lassie settled back onto the couch for a beauty nap while I chauffeured Lizzie back home. As both of them will tell you, it's anything but a dog's life.

"Ramona"

No man who has a cat can ever claim to be king of his castle. (No man who has a wife and children can ever make that claim, either, but that's another story.)

I found this out in 1989, when Sue and I moved with Katie and Lauren from an apartment to a condominium in Stamford, Connecticut. The girls, who longed for a "real pet," had grown tired of goldfish whose life expectancy was approximately as long as the Super Bowl halftime show. They wanted something that could return their affection, that had some semblance of intelligence, that would respond to their every command. True, they already had me. But they wanted something more. Specifically, they wanted a cat.

So, on an overcast Saturday, we went to the Humane Society and saw cats of every conceivable make and model. Asking not one child but two children, ages 9 and 7, to pick out the pet of their dreams borders on cruelty, not necessarily to the children, who would gladly devote their lives to such an endeavor, or to the cat, who couldn't care less because there's a sucker born every minute, but most definitely to the parents.

Ultimately, the decision was in my hands. Or, more accurately, on my feet. That's because one little kitten, a black and white cutie of almost unimaginable softness, climbed out of her box, scampered over to me and began to rub up against my size 11 sneakers. When I picked her up, she snuggled against my cotton shirt and purred contentedly. It would be years before she showed me such affection again. Of course, I couldn't have known that. But it was late, the girls were hopelessly confused and I was hooked, so I announced, "This is the one."

Katie named her Ramona, after Ramona Quimby, the title character in a series of books by children's author Beverly Cleary. It was a monumental misnomer: Ramona, the fictional 8-year-old girl, was charming, lively and smart; Ramona, the real-life 8-week-old cat, was grumpy, boring and stupid. But the girls were happy. Sue and I were, too, because for all her mental deficiencies, Ramona quickly learned how to use the litter box. I like to think she followed my example because, of course, I was already housebroken.

Ramona became internationally famous in 1992 as a charter member of "Who's Who of Animals." Here was her entry in that prestigious publication:

"Ramona Geraldine Zezima

"Stamford, Connecticut

"Ramona is a 3-year-old domestic house cat. She is small, sleek and coal black except for her white paws and whiskers and a white hourglass patch on her throat and chest. Ramona's greatest claim to fame is that she is even dumber than our goldfish, Pumpkin, out of whose bowl she likes to drink. A recent intelligence test pitting Ramona and a loaf of Wonder Bread proved inconclusive. She also is lazy, aloof and virtually unemployable. Still, we all love her because, frankly, we are only human."

Ramona's cushy lifestyle as a pampered princess who rarely deigned to associate with commoners ended in 1995 with the arrival of the newest member of the family, a puppy named Lizzie. Sensing competition, Ramona finally began warming up to us.

Her miraculous transformation into an affectionate sweetheart continued in 1998, when we moved to Long Island, New York, and got another cat, Kitty, who then had her own kitties, Bernice and Henry, all of whom ignored Ramona, who was only too happy to reciprocate and focus her attention on us.

Just before her Sweet 16th birthday party, Ramona began emitting a series of loud, strange, agonizing cries that sounded a lot like me when I get out of bed in the morning. Sue didn't help matters when she shook her head sadly and said, "It's her time."

I rushed to the animal hospital with Ramona, who sat calmly as the veterinarian checked her teeth and, at the other end, took her temperature. Then he listened to her heart and began feeling her stomach. "Have you watched her when she uses the litter box?" he asked.

"I don't make a habit of it," I replied. "Why?"

"Because," the vet announced, "she's constipated."

"You mean I worried myself sick over this stupid animal, thinking she was at death's door, and the only thing wrong with her is that she can't have a bowel movement?" I said incredulously.

"I'm afraid so," said the vet.

The bill: $165.10. The prescription: a stool softener.

Our first "real pet" enjoyed good health for four more years, until about three weeks ago, just a few days before the end. She was two months shy of her 20th birthday.

For two decades, Ramona had us all wrapped around her little paw. She lived on her own terms and was loved unconditionally.

I guess she was pretty smart after all.

CHAPTER 5:
"IT'S A GUY THING"

"Leaving No Stone Unpassed"

There comes a time in a man's life when he finds himself between a rock and a hard place. Unfortunately, my time came a couple of weeks ago, the hard place was a hospital gurney and the rock turned out to be a kidney stone.

According to several trained nurses, who not only took very good care of me but also happen to be women, having a kidney stone is the male equivalent of childbirth, the main difference being that you don't have to put the stone through college.

Now that I have miraculously survived the ordeal, I can say with great relief and a mind still clouded by painkillers that what I actually had was a kidney boulder, a large, jagged chunk of calcium and perhaps asphalt that was eventually removed with the help of Roto-Rooter and is now being analyzed to see if it contains either deadly bacteria or some form of Martian life. After it comes back from the lab, Lauren, who is on the cutting edge of fashion, wants to have it made into a ring.

This sad chapter in the annals of medicine began at 6 o'clock one weekday morning when I woke up (always an encouraging sign) with a sharp pain in my left side. At first I thought I had managed to pull a muscle in my sleep. But Sue, who usually wakes up with a pain in the neck, said I was being ridiculous, which meant, of course, that nothing was wrong.

Then I thought I was having an attack of appendicitis. But that diagnosis was dismissed when I was told that the appendix, the only organ in my body more useless than my brain, is located on the other side. This is why I never went to medical school.

Even as the pain intensified, I hesitated to call the doctor or go to the emergency room. And for a very good reason: What if it turned out to be gas?

Fortunately, Sue, taking pity on me, called the doctor, who was not in yet but was being paged and would call back in five minutes. I couldn't wait. Two minutes later, mooing in agony, I begged my wife to take me to the hospital.

Naturally, we got stuck in traffic. This did not deter Sue, who displayed the driving skill of a NASCAR champion in rushing me to the emergency room, where I not only was diagnosed with a kidney stone, but I also, thank God, was given drugs.

Then I was taken to X-ray and given an IVP, a procedure in which your system is flooded with a dye that, to use sophisticated medical terminology, looks like grape Kool-Aid. Although it showed the size (42 regular) and location (Stamford, Connecticut) of my stone, it also prompted another pain attack so severe that, in my delirium, I actually asked to be shot.

It was at this point that I was introduced to my new best friend, Mr. Demerol. This is just one man's opinion, but that's a damn fine product. If the person who invented it did not win the Nobel Prize, there is no justice.

Then the urologist who was called in for the case told me that, in romancing the stone, one of three things would happen:

1. This, too, would pass.
2. It would have to be surgically removed.
3. He'd have to blast.

Because Option No. 2 involved using a scope the length of a boa constrictor and Option No. 3 involved blowing the stone to smithereens with a laser, the doctor opted for No. 1. Personally, I thought it was a wise choice.

The next morning, after the stone had dropped a bit, I was sent home with a strainer that looked like one of those little paper party hats, except not as colorful. I was supposed to use it to void where not prohibited by law.

Six hours later, I was back in the emergency room, where I was given a shot of morphine that did not, I regret to say, have any effect whatsoever. Then I was taken up to the same room I had the day before and was visited by Virginia, the nice lady in the next room, who did a double take and said, "You're back?"

Yes, I was. Fortunately, I also was visited later that evening by Mr. Demerol. A priest came in, too, which frankly had me worried.

The following morning, I had the scope job, which I approved only on the condition that I would be knocked out, even if it meant being hit over the head with a croquet mallet. By that time, I was painfully familiar with the common medical term "slight discomfort."

Even though I have had to drink so much water that I am starting to sprout gills, and my backside looks like a pincushion, everything came out fine.

Now that I am on the gravel-paved road to recovery, I must say that the care I received from everyone at St. Joseph Medical Center in Stamford was excellent. And my medicine man, Dr. Vincent Tumminello, ace urologist, is a credit to his profession.

I would say that they left no stone unturned, but it hurts just thinking about it.

"A Briefing by Inspector No. 122"

I recently had a brief encounter with a woman who really got into my underwear. She was a pretty hot number.

No. 122, to be exact.

The whole scandalous affair began one weekday morning when I went to a local department store to buy a value pack of Hanes men's briefs, which, as the discriminating consumer no doubt knows, are made of "100 percent cotton preshrunk fabric" and are "unconditionally guaranteed."

In man's never-ending battle against wedgies, this is very important.

So I bought the underwear and, being rather modest by nature, waited until I got home to try it on.

When I opened the pack, however, I noticed a small piece of paper on which was printed the following information: "This garment inspected by 122."

My first thought was: Why don't I take off my pants before I try on my new underwear?

Then I wondered: Who is Inspector No. 122?

Immediately I recalled the famous Inspector No. 12, the feisty, grandmotherly, no-nonsense woman in the old Hanes television commercials who, like a master drill sergeant, would hold up a pair of men's briefs and bark, "They don't say Hanes until *I* say they say Hanes!"

But that was so long ago I was sure Inspector No. 12 had either retired or gone to that big laundry basket in the sky.

Then I imagined a younger woman – dark, mysterious, sultry – running her fingers through my briefs and purring, "These are disgusting."

Then I thought: What if Inspector No. 122 is a guy? "Yo, pal," I could hear him bellow approvingly. "Nice zooms!"

In an effort to learn the true identity of Inspector No. 122, I called Hanes at its corporate headquarters in Winston-Salem, North Carolina. The first thing I found out is that Hanes is owned by Sara Lee. Of course, nobody doesn't like Sara Lee. I just hope the pastry and panty divisions don't get their buns mixed up.

Anyway, I spoke with a very nice woman named Sherry Hauber, who is executive secretary to both Paul Snyder, vice president and general manager of male underwear, and Carol Mabe, vice president and general manager of Hanes Her Way panties.

"I'm definitely into drawers, one way or another," Sherry said.

She then connected me to Mr. Snyder, who promised to go undercover (he said it, not me) to track down Inspector No. 122.

A short time later, I knew her name: Diane Peoples.

"Was that your underwear I inspected?" she asked when I reached her at the Hanes Distribution Center in Davie County, North Carolina.

"Size 34," I told her. "You did a real nice job."

This is nothing new for Diane, a 14-year Hanes veteran who understandably takes great pride in her work.

"I don't think I ever said when I was a little girl, 'I want to be an underwear inspector when I grow up,' but I do view it as a big responsibility," she said.

What does Diane look for during her careful inspections, or "spot checks," of men's underwear?

"Pretty much the same things you would look for, only closer," she said. "I make sure there are no loose strings or threads, no holes in the garments, no loose seams and no discoloration."

What about spots? After all, these are spot checks.

"Sometimes I do spot one," Diane said with a sigh. "I also have to make sure that the waistband is properly attached. That's very important."

So are the right measurements.

"I often get out a tape measure to check width, length and the size of the leg holes," said Diane, adding that properly attached waistbands and comfortably snug leg holes are what help prevent wedgies.

"That's the bottom line," I said.

"Please, no cracks," Diane replied dryly. "I've heard all the underwear jokes."

Even so, she said that her main mission as Inspector No. 122 is to make sure everyone is fully covered.

"I myself appreciate it," said Diane, who, as you might expect, wears Hanes Her Way panties.

I wouldn't know anything about that, of course, but Sue would. When I told her that another woman – a married woman, no less – had gone through my briefs, Sue shrugged and said, "I hope she had a good time."

Then she told me to get my dirty underwear off the floor. Talk about getting caught with your pants down.

"Uncovering Victoria's Big Holiday Secret"

I like to keep abreast of the latest fashion trends, so I went to the bank to apply for a loan so I could buy Sue the new $10-million Millennium Bra from Victoria's Secret.

I couldn't help noticing this glittering garment because we get about a dozen Victoria's Secret catalogs in the mail every week. Although they are addressed to Sue, I have it on good authority (Becky Finn, who not only is the mother of Lauren's best friend, Lauren Finn, but is vice president of the Victoria's Secret catalog) that they are really meant for me. Too bad they don't have anything in my size.

Becky has even arranged for me to attend a couple of Victoria's Secret fashion shows in New York City. The first time I went, Sue circled an item in the catalog – "the sleeveless tank with the retro point collar ($19)" – and asked if I could place an order for her.

At the end of the show, I buttonholed Ingrid, the model who was wearing the item in the catalog, and asked if I could order one.

"Sure!" she chirped. "But not with me. Would you like an autograph?"

Ingrid took my pen and, over the picture of her in the sleeveless tank with the retro point collar, wrote: "Buy it. Ingrid."

It was then that I learned Victoria's Secret: No discounts.

So I knew the moment I saw supermodel Heidi Klum sporting the Millennium Bra on the cover of the Christmas Dreams and Fantasies catalog that I would have to pay full price.

And I'm sure it's worth every penny. As it says on page 3 of the catalog, next to a photo of Heidi in her cups: "The $10 Million Millennium Bra: The ultimate gift to celebrate the beginning of the century. Our satin demi bra and panty are encrusted with over 2,000 exquisite diamonds and diamond-cut sapphires, all of the finest cut and quality and all showcased in platinum star settings. One strap glitters '2000' in diamond-shaped platinum; the other is a simple strand of diamonds. This ultimate fantasy gift: $10,000,000."

This got me thinking: Is the price the same for everyone? If not, how much would Dolly Parton have to pay? To justify the cost, would a woman have to risk catching cold or even being arrested by walking around with her brassiere showing? How would you clean it? And what about having it appraised? Would a woman have to go to a jeweler, rip open her blouse and ask, "How much are these worth?"

But the most important question was: Would my bank loan me $10 million to buy a bra?

To find out, I went to the nearest branch office with the Victoria's Secret catalog and spoke with a very nice "customer relationship specialist" named Joanne.

"People come in to get loans for cars, houses, college, medical bills – sometimes the medical bills are for things that would go into a bra, if you know what I mean – but I've never had anyone come in for a loan to buy a bra," Joanne said.

She said I could apply for one of two kinds of loans: a secured loan or a personal loan.

"A secured loan means you already have the money in the bank," Joanne said. "Do you have $10 million?"

"No," I admitted. "If I did, I wouldn't need a loan."

"A personal loan," she explained, "means you have no collateral. You would have to provide three years of financial statements – personal and business – to show what you're worth."

"Scientifically speaking," I said, "I'm worth about $1.98."

"In order to get a loan for $10 million," Joanne said, "you'd have to be worth $100 million."

"Does this mean I don't qualify?" I asked.

"Not even close," said Joanne.

Just out of curiosity, I asked Joanne if she would wear the Millennium Bra. "No," she said flatly. "My birthday suit is free. Why should I spend $10 million on a bra?"

"Suppose your husband wanted to buy it for you," I said.

"He doesn't have the money," Joanne replied. "And I wouldn't give him a loan."

But she did give me some valuable financial advice. She started thumbing through my catalog and opened to page 61. There stood Heidi Klum, who is all over the place, in a silver chemise ($25) with a lace-trimmed, knee-length matching wrap ($35).

"You don't have to have a body like hers to wear something like that," Joanne said. "It's classy. And it's very inexpensive. Throw in some moisturizer and you're in for under $100. The rest you can give to charity."

I thanked Joanne and told her I had decided to forget about the Millennium Bra and instead get my wife a flannel nightgown for Christmas.

"And a pair of fuzzy slippers," Joanne added with a wink. "Women love them."

After all, she agreed, it's the thought that counts.

"A Real Gem"

I'm the very model of the modern man. And I proved it when I made my debut as a model at a women's jewelry show.

This sparkling event was hosted by my sister Susan, an independent representative for Silpada Designs Jewelry. She wanted to celebrate the opening of her business with a party where she could showcase her merchandise and where the invited guests – ladies only – could chat, laugh, gossip, try on jewelry, place orders, nibble on snacks, sip coffee and otherwise behave in a sophisticated and civilized manner that did not involve beer and belching, thus distinguishing it from a gathering of guys.

Sue couldn't make it because she was working, so I decided to crash the party, which was held at my parents' house, and look for something to buy for her.

In exchange for being the only man except my father, who lives there and couldn't very well be kicked out even though his jewelry consists of cufflinks and tie clasps, I agreed to be the model.

Amy, a Silpada representative who was sponsoring Susan, who was hosting the party even though the hostess was actually my mother (there is never this kind of confusion when guys get together to watch a game), predicted that I would be the life of the party.

That sentiment was echoed by the guests, who included my sister Elizabeth and Susan's daughter, Whitney, who is 11. The other guests were Linda, Sally, Joanne, Patty and Kathy.

"You will be good for business," Amy told me.

"I've been giving Susan the business since we were kids," I replied, "so I'm happy to help."

The first of the many compliments I received was from Amy, who said that my baby-blue-and-white, vertically striped shirt was "very slimming." She didn't say anything about my jeans and sneakers, but I could tell she was impressed by my sense of style.

Then I tried on my first piece of jewelry, a beautiful garnet lariat. I swept out of the bathroom and sashayed across the rug in the finished basement, turning gracefully so the ladies could get the full effect. When they applauded, I knew my modeling debut was going to be a smash.

"Garnet is my birth stone," I announced, prompting cheers. "It's better than a kidney stone," I added, prompting groans.

Next Amy gave me a matching garnet bracelet, but it was too small, so she added an extender. She winked and said something about putting me in handcuffs. I blushed. The women giggled. And I thought guys were bad.

To complete the set, Amy gave me a pair of earrings. I don't have pierced ears, although I do have a hole in my head, so she had to clip them to my earlobes. One earring stayed on but the other kept falling off. "They must be from the van Gogh collection," I said to Amy, who attached the earrings to my collar.

"You look fabulous," Joanne commented.

"Sometimes a boy just likes to feel pretty," I replied.

After taking off the ensemble, I donned a gorgeous turquoise necklace. "It's you," Linda said. "But you need something to go with it."

"How about a silver chain?" Kathy suggested.

Sally spotted an item that definitely was not part of the collection – a leash my parents keep for my dog, Lizzie, and Elizabeth's dog, Lucie, both of whom also attended the party. The leash had a silver chain.

"That's for later," Amy said, nodding toward me and eliciting hoots from the guests.

"Ladies, please!" I protested. "What would my wife think?"

Actually, she thinks I'm wonderful because I bought her the turquoise necklace. My mother got the garnet lariat. The other women looked through the catalog and made plenty of purchases.

"Thanks to you," Susan told me afterward, "the show was a huge success. You should be a model again."

It looks like I'll get the chance because Sue has agreed to host a jewelry party. Being a sex symbol is a tough job, but somebody's got to do it.

"Baby Face Zezima"

Baby face, I've got the cutest little baby face.

Those are the lyrics I am singing to myself these days, not just because I smell like a baby, but because I look like one.

That is what I was told when I went to the makeup counter at a department store after finding out that wearing makeup is the latest fashion trend among men.

I had heard about it when I went to that same store with Sue to buy cologne.

According to a recent story by The Associated Press, baby powder scent is popular in women's perfumes. As a man who not only has been called a big baby but is often told to take a powder, I wondered if the same were true for men's cologne.

"It's true that baby powder scent is popular with women because they love that new baby smell," said a fragrance specialist named Phyllis. "I imagine men feel the same way."

"I have two daughters who are all grown up, but I can still remember what they smelled like when they were babies," I said. "I don't think I want to smell like that."

"He never wanted to change their diapers," Sue explained.

Phyllis nodded knowingly and introduced me to Michael, the fragrance manager, who took me to the men's counter to see if there was anything that would make me smell like a freshly changed infant. After being sprayed with an array of colognes, I picked Touch by Burberry, which is aptly named because it has a touch of baby powder.

"Baby powder is good," Michael said, "but the real trend among men these days is makeup. A lot of guys are buying it. It's not for me, but if you want to look better, go for it."

That's what I did a few days later, when I went back to the store, this time without Sue, and headed for the makeup counter, where I met Jenna, a makeup artist, and Keri, a beauty analyst.

"I sell a lot of self-tanners to guys," Keri said. "One application lasts for a week and makes you look bronzed."

"It also covers up acne," noted Jenna, who is 19.

"My zits cleared up a long time ago," I said.

"You have very healthy-looking skin," said Keri, who is 23. "And no wrinkles."

"Except for these crow's-feet around my eyes," I remarked. "It looks like a flock of birds landed on my face."

"Those aren't crow's-feet," Keri assured me. "They're smile lines."

I smiled and said, "I guess I don't need plastic surgery."

Keri and Jenna smiled. They didn't have crow's-feet. But they did have a color chart they used as a guide to determine my skin tone.

"On this spectrum," Keri pointed out, "you are in the red and orange range. They're warm colors, which means you would look good wearing brown, green or gold."

I was wearing blue, but I guess it didn't matter.

Keri then dipped a buff brush into a small jar of powdery makeup and started applying it to my face. "This helps cover pores and blemishes," she said, "but you really don't have any. Your face is very clear. And very smooth."

"Like a baby's?" I asked.

"Yes," said Keri, adding that some guys buy makeup to cover blotches and even use eyeliner. "They want to hide their imperfections," she said.

"It's probably a clever rouge to attract women," I guessed.

"I think that's the reason," said Keri, who handed me a mirror.

"I don't notice any difference," I said.

"You don't need makeup," said Jenna, who saved me a lot of money because the stuff that Keri applied costs $32.50 per 0.31-ounce jar.

When I got home, I told Sue about my makeup session. "I look like a baby and I smell like a baby," I said.

Sue nodded and replied, "So when are you going to grow up?"

"Oh, Give Me a Foam Where the Beer Is My Own"

Of all the beers on the market, there is only one that is guaranteed to go down smooth and come back up the same way.

You tried the others first, now try the worst: Jerry's Nasty Ale.

Yes, beer lovers, in finally jumping onto the home-brewing bandwagon, which I did immediately after falling off the wagon, I have created a beer so distinctive, so surprising, so absolutely awful that it is barely fit for human consumption. This means that it is better than most of the major light beers.

I decided to brew my own beer after discovering that I was one of approximately six adult males in the United States who had not yet done so. Also, I was inspired by my friend Tim Lovelette, whose homemade beer not only was the best I had ever tasted, but had the powerful effect of destroying virtually all of my cognitive functions for a period of about 48 hours.

Besides, beermaking is a proud tradition dating back to the Middle Ages, when a bunch of guys invented a beverage that made them belch, tell dirty jokes and go to the bathroom a lot while creating the sad illusion that they were irresistible to women. It also led to professional football.

So I went to a store called Maltose Express, which sells home-brewing supplies, and purchased all the ingredients and equipment I would need to make two cases of Jerry's Nasty Ale. This included a five-gallon plastic brewing pot, a five-gallon carboy, a bag of crystal grains, six pounds of malt syrup, a bag of Irish moss, a packet of yeast, a bag of corn sugar, a siphoning hose, 48 bottles, 48 bottle caps, one bottle capper, a thermometer and an instruction book. Cost: $85.

"I'm sure your beer will come out great," said Tess Szamatulski, who owns the store with her husband, Mark. Tess added that I couldn't do any worse than the guy whose daughter put dog food in his first batch of beer. Maybe he should have called it Curs Light.

My brewing adventure began one lazy Friday afternoon as I stood in the kitchen, reading the instructions and, for inspiration, slugging down a cold beer made by what is now a rival brewery.

The first thing I had to do was crush the grains, which I did by dumping them into a popcorn bowl and whacking them with a ball peen hammer. Then I had to steep them in half a gallon of pure natural tap water (Jerry's Nasty Ale contains only the finest ingredients) at medium heat for 15 minutes. After that, I strained the water into the brewing pot, poured a quart of fresh water over the grains (which by that time were soggy and disgusting) and threw them away.

Next I had to boil a gallon and a half of water in a stainless steel pot, pour in the malt syrup and the Irish moss, and regulate the heat to make sure it didn't boil over, which would have been a disaster, not only because the bubbling concoction bore an eerie resemblance to "The Blob," but because the fumes made the whole house smell like a bucket of dead fish.

After removing the pot from the stove and letting it cool in the sink, which was filled with ice water to give my beer that special cold-filtered taste, I waited 10 minutes, strained the stuff into the brewing pot and threw out the leftover moss (aside from the food at college, it was the most revolting gunk I have ever seen). Then I put in the yeast, brought the brewing pot down to the basement and let the beer ferment for four days.

After dinner one night, I siphoned the brew, which was brown and cruddy, into the glass carboy and let it sit (or possibly stand) for a couple of weeks.

On a quiet Sunday morning, before I had even had breakfast, I went downstairs to bottle my beer. I had to siphon it back into the brewing pot, and pour in three-quarters of a cup of corn sugar and half a quart of boiled water, before I could siphon it into the bottles. Not being a master siphoner, I swallowed a fair amount of the stuff and spilled even more. By the time I had finished bottling, my eyes were spinning like pinwheels.

A week later, I put a six-pack of my beer in the refrigerator and waited a couple of hours. Then I poured the first bottle of Jerry's Nasty Ale into a frosty mug, took a deep breath and sipped. I expected it to taste like kerosene that had been run through a moose, only not as smooth. It didn't.

"Mmmm, this is good!" Sue said after she had taken a swig.

"It's got a nice flavor," my friend Bruce commented.

And my neighbor Ralph exclaimed, "Hey, I like it!" Then he belched.

Actually, the stuff isn't too bad. That's why I think Jerry's Nasty Ale could soon be America's favorite beer. Then millions of beer lovers across the country will be saying: "It's Jerry Time!"

"I Stooge to Conquer"

I may never win the Pulitzer Prize, which is journalism's highest honor, because I engage in the type of journalism you are reading right now. It is a safe bet I will never be awarded the Nobel Prize for Literature, Peace, Physics or anything else, although if they had a category for parallel parking I might have a chance. And I certainly have no hope of ever receiving an Emmy, an Oscar, a Tony or even a ribbon from the American Legion.

But these awards would pale compared to the honor I recently received from an organization that has recognized me for the thing I apparently do best. Therefore, I take great pride in announcing that I have been chosen first runner-up in the National Curly Howard Sound-Alike Contest.

Yes, fellow knuckleheads, it's true. All those years of watching the Three Stooges on television, of having my mind, which is a terrible thing to waste, numbed by the antics of three men whose chief claim to fame was their propensity for hitting each other with crowbars and banana cream pies, have finally paid off. Literally. Even as you read this, I am eagerly awaiting a check for $100 from Phone Programs Inc., the New York-based company that sponsored the contest.

Here's how it happened. From July 11 to September 3, Phone Programs, in conjunction with Norman Maurer Productions Inc. and Columbia Pictures Industries Inc., ran a national Three Stooges telephone program. The idea was to get birdbrains like me to call the special 900 number and, for $2 for the first minute and $1 for each additional minute, play the hotline's Three Stooges Trivia Game and participate in the Curly Sound-Alike Contest.

Because my time and money are so valuable, I called as soon as I heard about it.

The program was actually a recording that allowed callers to respond to questions by pressing buttons on their touch-tone phones. Although I correctly answered all three questions in the Stooge trivia game, which just goes to show the value of a college education, my name was not among those drawn in the winners' lottery, so I was not eligible to win the grand prize: a car called, appropriately enough, the Stoogemobile.

I had better luck in the Curly Sound-Alike Contest, in which participants were required to do Curly imitations into the phone. I forget exactly what I did (I wouldn't repeat it anyway because my boss is within earshot), but I'm pretty sure it was something along the lines of "Soitenly!" and "Nyuk, nyuk, nyuk!" I think I even did some sound effects, though I definitely stopped short of hitting myself with either a crowbar or a banana cream pie.

The recordings of three other contestants were played back for each hotline caller, who was then asked to vote for the best one. Of the literally thousands of calls that Phone Programs received, my recording was voted second-best in the entire country.

"Congratulations!" chirped Stephanie Souflis, project manager for Phone Programs, when she called to tell me the good news. Stephanie, who would not reveal the name of the winner, probably because he is an inmate somewhere, said that "all sorts of people" entered the contest. "We had everyone from women to little kids," she said. "We could even make out certain ethnic accents." (Just imagine: "Buenos dias! Nyuk, nyuk, nyuk!")

Of course, modesty prevents me from being too boastful, mainly because this is not the kind of thing a middle-age man likes to brag about, but it could work to my advantage. I can see the job offers roll in when I put this prestigious honor on my resume: "As a National Curly Sound-Alike winner, Mr. Zezima, you are perfectly qualified to be chief of surgery at this hospital."

Before long, all the best clubs will be vying for my membership. I also expect my suavity and newfound fame to attract scores of admiring women.

Me: "Hiya, toots!"

Admiring woman: (Slap!)

Eventually, the Pulitzer and Nobel committees will have no choice but to admit that a person of my obvious talent should not go unrecognized. This would give me a chance to realize my lifelong dream of starting a pie fight at an awards banquet. Just like Curly. Nyuk, nyuk, nyuk!

"The Lord of the Ringtones"

At the risk of being sued by J.R.R. Tolkien, which is a remote possibility considering he is, at the present time, dead, I am going to title my autobiography "The Lord of the Ringtones." That's because I have just become the last man in America to get a cell phone.

I have always hated cell phones for two understandable reasons: (a) they don't work and (b) if they do, it is at 2 a.m., when Lauren's cell phone goes off and wakes everyone in the house except, of course, Lauren.

But this is the 21st century, and Sue, Katie and Lauren have been trying to get me out of the Middle Ages, where I have been living because I am (physically, if not mentally) middle-aged. So they bought me a cell phone.

I had never seen the point of having one because cellular technology is so primitive that it would be more efficient to open the window and shout to the person you are trying to talk with. No wonder the entire cellular telephone industry is based on a popular corporate slogan: "Can you hear me now?" This is a shocking indication that even the phone company doesn't expect the stupid thing to work. Imagine if other industries used this tactic.

Cardiologist (to patient): "Is it beating now?"

Car salesman (to customer on test drive): "Do the brakes work now?"

Cell phone user (punching man in TV commercial): "Can you feel it now?"

I had always thought that the only good reason to have a cell phone was to find the house phone, a portable that Lauren sometimes uses and invariably leaves somewhere in the house, making it impossible to locate unless she uses her cell phone to call our home number.

Now that I have my own cell phone, however, I am beginning to change my outlook. Programming the phone was an adventure in itself. With the help of Lauren, Katie and Sue, I entered a wondrous world where all things are possible except actual conversation.

First, I had to choose a ringtone, which is what I will hear when the phone bleeps, or blips, or bloops, or whatever it does when someone calls. Among my choices were Bee Boogie, Chicken Dance, In the Groove, Just Jazzy, Exhilaration and Tap Dance. One was more annoying than the next.

"Isn't there a simple ring?" I wanted to know.

Lauren, who was programming everything for me because I couldn't comprehend the 134-page user guide, shook her head. I asked her to play them all again. And again.

"Make up your mind!" Katie said. So I chose Tap Dance, which goes like this: "Do-do-do, do do do, do-do-do-do."

Then I called the house phone, not only to find out where it was, but to see if my cell phone worked. The phone rang. Sue got up to get it. "Don't answer it," Lauren said. "It's Dad."

Finally, the true test. I asked Sue to call my cell phone on her cell phone. She sat in one room. I went into the next room. "Go ahead," I shouted. Sue dialed my new number. My cell phone rang. I answered it. Here is a direct transcript of our conversation.

Me: "Hello."

Sue: "Hi."

Me: "Hi."

Sue: "What?"

Me: "Hi."

Sue: (Inaudible.)

Me: "I can't hear you."

Sue: "What?"

Me: "Thanks for the call."

Sue: "You're welcome. Can I hang up?"

Me: "What?"

Sue: "Come in here."

Me: "What?"

Sue: "What?"

Me: "Can you hear me now?"

"Bumper Cars"

In the nearly four decades since I got my driver's license, during which time I've compiled an excellent record of driving people crazy, I have learned that men are prohibited by law from asking for directions. That is why navigation systems were invented.

Unfortunately, there are some men for whom this sophisticated technology doesn't work. I know because I recently ran into one.

At an intersection.

In my car.

I took this crash course in masculine geography when I crashed into a car that cut in front of me. As I was cruising through a green light, traveling well under the speed limit, the driver of the other car suddenly turned left because, as he explained later, his GPS told him to.

His GPS must have stood for Guy Positioning System, designed to help guys who don't know where the hell they are going, but like most guys it had a poor sense of direction. I say so because it told the other driver, whom I will call "John" because that is his real name, to go the wrong way down a one-way street.

In that one terrible instant, my life flashed before my eyes. I am sorry to admit that it was pretty dull. Then, BAM! It was like playing bumper cars at an amusement park except that it wasn't so amusing because my car was parked in the left lane with me inside, an airbag spewing acrid smoke after deploying against my head.

Later on, after family, friends and co-workers had been told of this little mishap, my two sisters showed great sympathy for my plight with words of comfort. "I always wondered what would happen if an airbag deployed against an airhead," Susan said. To which Elizabeth added, "You mean an airbag against a windbag."

Obviously nothing happened because I was able to walk away without a scratch. I wish I could say the same for my car.

Amid the mayhem of honking horns and rubbernecking motorists, I looked around for the other car and found it across the street, sitting in front of a truck at the corner. The impact had spun the car around so it was, unlike its original direction, facing the right way.

"I'm sorry," John blurted after he rolled down the window. "It's all my fault."

"Are you OK?" I asked.

"Yes," he said. "Are you?"

"Yes," I replied.

"I don't know what happened," John moaned. "I was looking at my GPS and it told me to turn left."

I helpfully pointed out to John that if he had been looking at the road instead of his GPS, he would have seen two things: (a) an arrow indicating he was going the wrong way and (b) me.

The crash occurred at 11:05 a.m. I am supposed to be to work by 11, but I was born more than three weeks past my due date and haven't been on time for anything since. This all happened about half a mile from my office in Melville, New York, which also is home to the Long Island National Cemetery. This means Melville is not a one-hearse town, as I found out when I got back in my car and attempted to pull out of the left lane and onto the right shoulder. I couldn't do so right away because there was a line of cars coming through. It was, incredibly, a funeral procession.

The guy driving the lead car, with the deceased in the back, rolled down his window and said, "Can I do anything for you?"

"Not today," I responded. "You'll have to wait before you get any business from me."

He smiled, rolled up the window and drove through. What he didn't know was that I was the late Jerry Zezima even before the accident.

When I went back to John's car, I noticed it had Connecticut plates. I asked him where he was from. "North Haven," he replied.

"Howdy, neighbor!" I said. "I'm originally from Stamford."

"Sorry we had to meet under these circumstances," said John, who told me that even though he lives in Connecticut, he works for a company that is headquartered in Canada but that his car is registered to another company in New Jersey.

"No wonder you need a GPS," I said.

Pretty soon a cop showed up and took statements from me and John, who admitted he was at fault and said his insurance company would take care of everything. But I still had to call mine to report the accident. Thank God Sue came to help me take care of everything.

Here's a tip for anyone with a driver's license: Never get into an accident because it is a pain, both figuratively and literally, in a lower portion of the anatomy. Even though my insurance company has been very good, I was at the accident scene for more than two hours, about half of which was spent on the phone talking with various claims people, not to mention the tow truck operator, who took my car to a garage where it is scheduled to undergo open-hood surgery. It has been estimated that there is a lot of damage but not enough to declare the vehicle totaled. Just my luck.

Speaking of a lower portion of the anatomy, mine was sore as a result of the accident, so that evening I went to the hospital as a precaution and had X-rays taken. Fortunately, I remembered my mother's words of wisdom, "Always wear clean underwear in case you are in an accident," and was wearing a pair of freshly laundered "I (Heart) Dad" boxer shorts. The X-rays, by the way, were negative.

Now that I have been in an accident and lived to tell about it, I have my own words of wisdom for all you guys out there: Never trust a GPS. If you don't know where you are going, break the law once in a while and ask for directions. Or, if at all possible, move over and let your wife drive.

CHAPTER 6:
"DOMESTIC DILEMMAS"

"Someone's in the Kitchen With a Paintbrush"

This week's Home Improvement Lesson is: How to paint your kitchen.

I happen to be a world-renowned expert on this subject, having spent most of my vacation doing a job I had successfully avoided for nearly three years.

This leads us to Painting Rule No. 1: Put it off for as long as possible. My neighbor tells me that she has been after her husband to paint their kitchen for the past NINE YEARS! And Sue thought I was bad.

Still, I hadn't picked up a paintbrush since Sue somehow persuaded me to paint the upstairs bathroom. Not long afterward, a water leak emanating from behind the shower in that very same bathroom trickled down through the kitchen ceiling, a large section of which had to be ripped out, rebuilt (not by me) and, of course, painted.

The painting finally got done last week.

This leads us to Painting Rule No. 2: Never take a vacation. Or never take one alone, because your wife, miffed that you were either too cheap or too inconsiderate to schedule a week off to coincide with her vacation, will exact terrible revenge by making you paint the kitchen.

As you will soon find out, painting the kitchen is even worse than painting the bathroom. There are two main reasons for this:

1. You have to use four miles of masking tape before you even begin to paint.

2. You must risk pulling virtually every muscle in your body so you can move both the refrigerator and the stove.

As you veteran painters no doubt know, masking tape is used to border the corners of any area you don't want to paint. For example, if you want to paint the ceiling, you must painstakingly put tape along the edge of the wall – or, as in some areas of our kitchen, the wallpaper or the wallpaper border – so you won't get paint on it. Same goes for cabinet tops, cabinet doors, counters, the floor, doorways, window frames, tile, the edge of the sink, the bottom of the wallpaper border and, just to be safe, the cat.

This took me a day and a half. And our kitchen is smaller than Martha Stewart's spice rack.

I completed the prep work by hauling the microwave into the living room, removing 32 baskets from the top of one cabinet, spackling the walls with a butter knife, and cleaning out the narrow floor area between the refrigerator and another cabinet, which was stuffed with the following items: 10 shopping bags, three bottles of tonic water, a pack of napkins, a bottle of apple juice, a bottle of wine, a gallon of wine, a can of olive oil, a bottle of Diet Coke, an empty maple syrup container, a watering can and a flyswatter.

Finally, it was time to paint. Sue wanted me to put on two coats, but I wore a T-shirt instead.

The trickiest part was painting the area around the ceiling fan, which is also where the kitchen lights are located. This meant that if I turned on the lights, I would be blinded. If I turned off the lights, I couldn't see what I was doing.

I worked with the lights on until I thought I smelled something burning. It turned out to be my hair, which had come in contact with a hot bulb. So I pulled one of two cords – the one I thought would turn off the lights – only to discover that I had accidentally turned on the fan, whereupon a whirling blade hit me in the head and knocked me forward.

Since I couldn't very well leap off the ladder and grab the fan, I braced myself by lunging, brush first, into the wall. Fortunately, it was an area I was supposed to paint anyway. It came out pretty nice.

I considered putting a small container of paint on each blade and turning on the fan at high speed so I could finish the job in record time, but thought better of it.

The rest of the job was pretty mundane except for the torturous task of moving the refrigerator and the stove. Removing several bottles of beer and promptly consuming them lightened not only the fridge but also my head. It made moving the stove a lot easier, too.

Unfortunately, I had to spend the better part of an hour cleaning several long tons of dirt and lint off the floor beneath both appliances.

Finally, after three long days of mess and misery, which were complicated by a viral infection that clogged my sinuses and – this is the only good part – rendered me immune to the paint fumes, the kitchen was finished.

"Nice job," Sue said approvingly. "Now when are you going to paint the living room?"

"The Heat's On"

The hot news in my house is that I am cool. Not cool personally because Sue and the girls have said for years that I am the most uncool man in America. I am cool physically because I have just sweated the big stuff by installing an air conditioner in our bedroom window.

When Sue and I were looking for a house a few years ago, we were shown some of the most pathetic dumps east of the Mississippi, including one place that had no panels in the front door. There were just two thin vertical gaps. After turning sideways and squeezing through one of them to get into the house, I turned back around to our real estate agent and asked, "Is this what you call central air-conditioning?" She turned away and started talking with Sue.

Soon thereafter we found another real estate agent and bought a house that has panels in the front door but, alas, no central air-conditioning.

After suffering through some long, hot summers, Sue insisted I do something about the situation or she was going to give me the cold shoulder. So I broke down (due to overheating) and bought an air conditioner.

It is supposed to cool off the entire upstairs, but because the upstairs is too big to cool off with just one air conditioner, Sue really wants central air-conditioning, which costs thousands of dollars and is installed by professionals. An air conditioner costs considerably less but weighs about as much as a baby grand piano and has to be lugged upstairs and installed in the bedroom window by someone who not only isn't a professional, but hasn't the faintest idea what the hell he is doing.

That person would be me. And speaking of fainting, I almost did. That's because it was unbearably hot upstairs. You might think this was due to the scientific principle that heat rises. Not true. Heat doesn't rise. It just follows you around if you have to do some onerous household project like installing an air conditioner. I could have worked in air-conditioned comfort if only the air conditioner had been installed, but I couldn't until I had installed the air conditioner.

This is known as a Catch-22: If I didn't catch the air conditioner as it started to slide out the window, it would have fallen 22 feet to the ground below. And it may yet do so, but it will wait until I am under the window and will hit me on the head, with the tragic result that the air conditioner will be ruined and I will have to install a new one.

Just the thought makes me hot because installing one air conditioner is trouble enough.

I started with two tools: a screwdriver (we were out of orange juice, so I had the vodka straight) and, I am on the level about this, a level. I had to use the latter instrument to make sure the air conditioner was tilting toward the outside at just enough of an angle so water wouldn't drip into the bedroom but not so much that the chilling scenario envisioned above would come true.

First, though, I had to get the air conditioner out of the box (I accomplished this by dumping it onto my foot); attach a couple of doohickeys to the bottom; hoist it into the open window without having a massive coronary; screw the accordion shutters to the window frame; use two more tools (a saw and a hammer) to cut and nail a piece of wood to the windowsill because otherwise the air conditioner would have crashed to the floor; stuff strips of foam rubber into any cracks to keep the bugs from getting in and eating me alive while I sleep; and read the instruction manual to figure out how to program the stupid thing. This was the most difficult part because I neglected to follow Step 1 ("Plug it in").

Sue likes the air conditioner so much that she wants me to buy another one and put it in my office window so the rest of the upstairs can be cooled off.

At this point, I am ready to get central air-conditioning. To save thousands of dollars, I'll take the panels out of the front door.

"A Real Swinger"

If I had a hammock, I'd hammock in the morning, I'd hammock in the evening, all over my land. I sang this song so often that Sue, who threatened to hit me over the head with the tool referred to in the original lyrics, finally gave in and bought me one.

For a lazy man, a hammock is like a LaZBoy, the outdoor equivalent of an easy chair, except that it's not so easy to get into. I found this out when I put up my hammock with the intention of lying in it for hours and doing what I do best – nothing.

One of the great things about a hammock is that it doesn't come with instructions. Unlike other simple devices with instruction manuals that look like they were written by NASA, a hammock is basic: You attach each end to a tree or a post and get ready to relax. Unless, of course, the hammock is attached to a frame that must be assembled, in which case you will never relax because you will never get it assembled. And if you do, the frame will tip over and, assuming you are not killed, you will have to find a more level piece of land. This may entail moving to Kansas.

By sheer coincidence, in my backyard there are two posts: The Washington Post and the New York Post. By even sheerer coincidence, there are two other posts, each about six feet high, in a shady, secluded corner of the yard. They are made of wood, stand eight feet from each other and seem to get along well. I don't know why they are there (I think the original owner was a little kinky), but I do know that, unlike the trees in my yard, which are either too close together or too far apart, these posts are perfect for hammocking.

I used an electric drill my father gave me, either for household projects or in case I wanted to practice dentistry, to drill a hole into each post. I inserted a large hook screw into each hole, hung the metal ring at each end of my hammock onto the corresponding hook and – voila! (French for "watch out!") – I was ready to swing.

There was just one problem: I had to get into the hammock first. For a novice, this is like trying to slow-dance with a greased pig. (Talk about kinky.)

It is during this initial attempt that you recall what you were taught in school about Newton's Law of Gravity, which states: "If a person tries to get into a hammock with some Fig Newtons, gravity will cause the cookies to fall to the ground, followed closely by the person."

As a precaution, I did not bring Fig Newtons with me when I tried to get into my hammock. And I made an important discovery: I could fall to the ground without them.

This happened when I eased my derriere (French for "what you will land on when you try to get into a hammock") onto the edge and lifted my legs in a vain attempt to get the rest of me settled. The hammock did half a revolution and dumped me out. For the next 20 minutes, I waged a half-a-revolutionary war with the stupid thing (it could have said the same about me) with varying results: Sometimes I landed on my backside, other times I landed on my head.

Finally, I got the hang of it, after almost hanging myself, and then tried to find a comfortable position. The next thing I knew, I was on the ground again. Before you could say Jack Robinson, who was smart enough to buy a LaZBoy, I had learned how to get into my hammock without suffering life-threatening injuries.

Then came the really tough part: getting into it with a beer. Eventually I learned not to open my beer until I was settled.

Now that I have mastered my hammock, I spend many relaxing hours in it on nice sunny days when I really should be cutting the grass or doing household projects.

Sue may hit me over the head with that hammer yet.

"Withering Heights"

One of the things I discovered when I bought my house is that being a homeowner is the height of folly. This was frighteningly evident the first time I went up on the roof to clean the gutters and discovered that I am petrified of heights.

It doesn't help that I live in the Mount Everest of houses. To the untrained eye (I have two, so the house seems twice as high), it's a two-story Colonial, but for me that's high enough. All it took was one climb to realize I was over my head.

That's why I recently called in a specialist to help me get over my acrophobia, a Greek word meaning "Don't look down!" His name is Rob Disalvo. He's not a shrink (imagine bringing a couch up there) but a roofer I had hired to fix a leak around the skylight above the family room.

Originally, Sue wanted me to go up on the roof to see if I could solve the problem. Even though the skylight is above the first-floor addition, only about 10 feet off the ground, I hate being up there. I am afraid I will slip, fly off the roof, do a triple somersault that would win me a gold medal in the Olympics and land on my head, in which case I wouldn't get hurt. But it would be pretty embarrassing.

So you can imagine how I felt when I had to go up on the roof above the second floor, where I could practically see passengers with window seats on passing airplanes. Instead of getting used to being up there, I was more frightened every year, until I finally got smart (or, at least, less stupid) and bought gutter guards.

When my pathetic efforts to fix the skylight failed, I called Disalvo, who owns RGI Construction in Miller Place, New York. He came with his ace assistants, Brian Lavoie and Brian Hurst.

"We're going to cure you of your fear of heights," Disalvo promised.

"Or die trying," Lavoie added.

"Who's your next of kin?" Hurst asked.

"Very funny," I muttered as I slowly climbed a ladder that Lavoie held. When I got up to the low part of the roof, Disalvo explained what had to be done to the skylight. Then he said, "It's not so bad up here, is it?"

"I guess not," I replied with a weak smile.

"Good," he said. "Now we're going up to the highest part of the house."

This entailed climbing up to another low roof above the kitchen and the garage and, from there, making the last climb to the summit. It took me approximately as long as it would take a kindergartner to read "War and Peace."

When I was finally up there, I swore I could see the Great Wall of China, though it may just have been the fence surrounding my yard.

"We're only 24 feet off the ground," said Disalvo, who had taken measurements.

"That's 23 feet higher than I would like," I responded nervously.

To allay my fears, Disalvo and the two Brians told me stories of rooftop adventures, including the one about a co-worker who fell through a roof and climbed back up before anyone had noticed. Disalvo, 38, said he once walked off the back of a roof. "Accidentally," he noted. Hurst, 32, and Lavoie, 23, have had minor mishaps, too, but they haven't been hurt because they're careful and they use safety equipment.

"I actually like heights," said Lavoie. "There's nobody to bother you up here."

"Except Rob," Hurst pointed out.

"See what I have to put up with?" Disalvo said.

It was great putting up with all three of them, not just because they did a good job on the skylight, but because they really did lessen my fear of heights, mainly by helping me climb down.

Now that I am back on terra firma – and the firmer the terra, the better – I can honestly say that it was one of the high points of my life. And if Sue ever wants me to go back up there, she can call the roofers.

"Growing Pains"

Jerry, Jerry, quite contrary, how does your garden grow? Not too badly considering I am more of a vegetable than anything I've planted this year.

Actually, the little patch of earth on the side of the house is the first garden I have ever had. Sue, who has a green thumb (she really ought to see a doctor), could grow tomatoes in Death Valley. I, on the other hand, which has a dirty thumb, am responsible for making parts of our property look like that famous desert.

So when the only plant I could not kill, a gigantic butterfly bush, was removed earlier this year, I decided to put in herbs (nobody named Herb was harmed during planting) and various veggies (not including broccoli and zucchini, which I will consume only at the point of a gun) and turn the place into a Garden of Eatin'.

I was inspired to get into agriculture, which is the only culture I have, by President Barack Obama and his wife, first lady Michelle Obama, who recently planted a White House garden that is approximately the size of Rhode Island.

Mine is somewhat smaller (83 by 64 inches, to be exact), but you have to start somewhere, and I didn't think the Secret Service would let me do so outside the Oval Office.

I went with Sue to one of those home-improvement warehouses to pick out what I wanted to plant.

"Do you like squash?" she asked as we walked through the garden department.

"I'd rather play tennis," I replied.

Sue ignored the remark and suggested we get vegetables I would actually eat, which narrowed the choices considerably. They included tomatoes, eggplants, jalapeno peppers, bell peppers, string beans and cauliflowers. We also got parsley, as well as basil and rosemary. In fact, Basil, Rosemary and Herb are having a nice little menage a twine, which I am using to hold up the tomato plants.

The planting itself was pretty hard work. I was about to throw in the trowel when I realized I wouldn't see the fruits of my labors. And since tomatoes are also considered fruits, I wasn't taking any chances, even though they were tough rows to hoe.

Speaking of rows, I could have used a rowboat – or maybe even an ark – after we had what seemed like 40 days and 40 nights of rain, which nearly caused a flood of biblical proportions. Sue said it was God's way of telling me that I couldn't be trusted to water the garden.

I got the hint, however, and when the rain finally stopped, I began giving the garden a shower every evening. I give myself a shower every morning, but not outside.

To break up the monotony, I started talking to my tomato plants. But I stopped after I heard a report on the radio about how men can stunt the growth of their tomato plants when they talk to them. According to a study conducted by the Royal Horticultural Society in Surrey, England, tomato plants will respond to a woman's voice much better than they will to a man's and will grow up to an inch more when they hear soothing female sounds.

I thought only cauliflowers had ears, but I guess our world isn't called Mother Nature for nothing. When I told Sue about the study, she said, "Shall I go out to the garden and have a conversation with the tomato plants?"

She must have done so because we now have tomatoes the size of baseballs. (Imagine if it were basketball season.) I think the real reason the plants are doing so well, and haven't been affected by the current fungus that has ruined many tomato crops, is that I no longer tell them stupid jokes when I water the garden.

At any rate, because of my tender care, or perhaps despite it, my garden is growing just fine. We have had several delicious meals featuring string beans, jalapenos and parsley, and there will be plenty more when the tomatoes, eggplants, bell peppers and cauliflowers are ready to eat. Maybe then, if they're not too busy tending their own garden, we'll invite the Obamas over for dinner.

CHAPTER 7:
"THE MIDDLE AGES"

"The Big 5-Oh!"

Today's entry in the Old Boomer's Almanac: How to be 50 and live to tell about it.

I am happy to say that I recently reached this milestone with many of my vital functions – including, on most mornings, a pulse – intact.

As a member of the Baby Boom Generation, which means I still act like a baby even though the boom is over, I have begun to grow old gracefully, if not gratefully. Or maybe it's the other way around.

Anyway, being 50 doesn't bother me. You just have to put up with the jests of younger people (almost everyone else) who send you birthday cards like the one my daughter Lauren gave me. It read: "Turning 50? Don't worry, it's just like turning 40 ... only with diapers." On the inside, she wrote: "Happy birthday. I contacted AARP for you."

My daughter didn't actually contact AARP ("Do you think I was going to spend time on the phone with an old person?" explained Lauren, who is 22), but she did make me realize that I have reached a new stage in my life, the age at which people start getting stuff in the mail from AARP.

I started to think about the future, and my own mortality, and the fact that I couldn't find my glasses.

I wondered:

Will I find peace and fulfillment in the coming years?

Will there *be* any coming years?

Will my children put me in the Sunset Home for Clueless Parents?

Will I start driving 20 miles per hour with my left blinker on?

Where are my car keys?

And, most important, can I get a senior discount on a six-pack of beer?

To begin my quest for answers to these and other pertinent questions, I went to see Lois Aronstein, New York state director of AARP in Manhattan, who greeted me by saying, "Welcome to 50!"

"Thanks," I replied. "It's nice to be here."

Aronstein, who reached my milestone 10 years ago ("I'm 60 and proud of it"), said I am entering an "absolutely positive" time of life. "You have to think young and act young," she advised.

"No problem," I told her. "I'm shockingly immature."

"That's good," she said. "Internally, we are ageless. It's how old you feel that matters. Sometimes, I feel like I'm 25. Or 17." She paused, adding: "I'm single."

"I'm married," I confessed. "But we can still be friends."

Aronstein, who sounded relieved, said that baby boomers are "much more youthful and more active than our grandparents were at our age, and we live longer. There is a lot ahead. The key ingredients are health and a sense of humor."

One drawback to being older, Aronstein acknowledged, is that when it comes to accepting senior discounts, people have to decide whether to be vain or thrifty.

"I'm cheap," I told her. "Would I be eligible for senior discounts?"

"Well," Aronstein said, "usually, you have to be 60, or 62, or 65, depending on where you go. But I guess you could try."

So I went to the Port Jeff Beverage Center in Port Jefferson Station, New York, and asked manager Frank Stoutenburg if I could get a senior discount on a six-pack of beer. His answer was swift and concise: "No." Then he said, "You're 50; you're not dying. If you were dying, I'd give it to you for free."

Stoutenburg, who is 46, said he doesn't see turning 50 as a big deal. "I don't consider it a crisis," he said.

"Do you have any advice for me?" I asked.

"Yeah," Stoutenburg said. "Never grow up."

Words to live by. The question is, how long will I live? To find out, or at least to get an idea of what kind of shape I'm in, I went for a physical with Dr. Leonard Vinnick, who has a private practice in my hometown of Stamford, Connecticut.

The good news was that my blood pressure, heart rate and body weight are normal.

The bad news was that I'm a lean, mean lounging machine. In other words, I am dangerously sedentary.

"What do you do for exercise?" the doctor asked.

"I get up once a night to go to the bathroom," I replied.

"You'll have to do more than that," he said. Being physically active, Vinnick said, is important for people 50 and older.

"Get some exercise," he said. "And have sex. Vigorous sex keeps a man vibrant and young."

Best doctor's orders I ever heard! I couldn't wait to tell my wife. Fortunately, she concurred, so it was nice to get a second opinion.

Vinnick, who recently celebrated a milestone of his own (he turned 70), added: "And don't even contemplate retirement."

How could I when I was still contemplating ... exercise?

Nonetheless, some boomers don't feel young if they don't look young, so I sought counsel from someone whose job is to help people in general, and me in particular, look good: my barber, Maria Vieira, who works the first chair at Sam's Barber Shop in Port Jefferson, New York.

"I think people in their late 30s or early 40s are more concerned about how they look, especially if they have gray hair," Vieira said. "By the time you're 50, even if you're balding, you've pretty much accepted it."

I'm not balding yet, but I do have some gray hair, which I've pretty much accepted.

"It's very thick," said Vieira, who recently turned 40 and said it didn't bother her. She remembered one customer, however, to whom growing older mattered a great deal.

"This guy in his early 50s came in and said he had just bought a Ford Mustang," Vieira recalled. "I guess he was having a midlife crisis. He said he was stopped at a red light when this young guy pulled up alongside and looked at him as if to say, 'Look at that old man in that nice car.' Then, the customer said, 'I realized that old man was me.' So he came back to get his hair colored."

After a while, though, the customer let his hair go back to its natural gray.

"Like you," Vieira told me.

Speaking of older drivers, I wondered if my driving skills, never good to begin with, would deteriorate to the point where I would start driving with my blinker on. For insight, I spoke with Joe Valle, owner of the Stress Free Driving School in Bohemia, New York. "If you're going to make a turn, turn your blinker on," he said. "After you make a turn, turn your blinker off."

It sounded simple enough. Then again, some people, like me, are oblivious to what's going on around them.

"Here's the way I look at it," I said. "The only thing worse than being behind an old driver is being in front of a young one."

Valle, who said the worst drivers are in their 30s, had this advice for drivers young and old: "Be careful out there. You never know what's going to happen."

Not necessarily. I know what's going to happen to me because I went to the Psychic Gallery in Huntington Village, New York, for a tarot card reading by psychic Christine Evans.

For $50, I got a peek into my future. After Evans asked me to cut a deck of tarot cards into three piles, she spread them out and studied them. Then she looked up at me and smiled. "Your lifeline indicates that you will have a very long and very healthy old age."

Evans, who is 62, also predicted that I will end up in a very warm place.

"Do you mean I'm going to hell?" I asked nervously.

"No," she said. "Maybe California."

Evans concluded by saying that I have "a very bright future" and that, best of all, "your wife has no intention of trading you in."

Sue and I have been married for 26 years – more than half our lives – and have raised two beautiful and loving daughters who, with true familial devotion, are now threatening to put me in a home. Of course, they're just kidding.

I think.

The bottom line, boomers, is this: The 50s are a wonderful time of life, with so much to look back on and so much to look forward to. True, you still have to pay full price for beer, but look at the bright side: Like red wine, it's good for your heart.

Even if you can't live life as fast as you used to, you can still live it just as fully. So have fun, stay positive, be active, accept yourself for who you are, and never grow up.

And don't forget sex.

"One Tough Cookie"

As the father of two daughters who used to be Girl Scouts, as well as a man who is often caught with his hand in the cookie jar, I know something about the value of money.

What I know is that I don't have much now and probably won't have any after I retire if something isn't done about Social Security.

That is why I have come up with a brilliant plan to save the Social Security system: Raise money by selling Girl Scout cookies.

I was inspired after reading a newspaper story about a Long Island man who was ticketed in Brooklyn for helping his daughter sell Girl Scout cookies without a license. When Katie and Lauren were young, I helped them sell cookies all the time and I didn't have a license, either. I'm lucky I didn't go to prison.

Then it dawned on me that a lot of the money in this country is spent on Girl Scout cookies and school fundraisers. This is why parents never have any cash. So if only a fraction of the money collected by Girl Scouts could go toward Social Security, the system would never go bankrupt.

I ran the idea past Ken Lisaius, a White House spokesman whose favorite Girl Scout cookies are Tagalongs, and Lois Aronstein, president of the New York state chapter of AARP in Manhattan, who said she loves Thin Mints. Both thought I had come up with a foolproof plan. The proof is that a fool came up with it.

But what about the Girl Scouts? Would they be willing to go along? Would they let me take part in a cookie sale? Would they bail me out if I got arrested for selling cookies without a license?

To find out, I contacted the Girl Scouts of Suffolk County, which is based in Commack, New York, and has 42,000 girls in its scouting program.

Both Yvonne Grant, chief executive, and Eileen Driscoll, director of product sales, thought it was a great idea. "The sale of Thin Mints alone could save the system," Grant said, referring to her favorite cookies, which also are the best-selling of the eight varieties. "This not only could benefit seniors now," Driscoll added, "but the girls could be putting money away for their retirement. It's a win-win situation."

According to Driscoll, there are 2.7 million Girl Scouts in the United States, half of whom sell cookies. Each girl sells an average of 120 boxes a year. Considering that each box costs $3.50, that adds up to what Driscoll, who is much better at math than I am, calculated as "a lot of money!"

Fifty cents of every box sold goes back to the troop, so if some of the larger amount that now goes to the national Girl Scouts went instead to Social Security, the system would be, pardon the expression, rolling in dough. Driscoll and Grant enthusiastically agreed, but not without a collective moan.

Although my plan still needs the approval of the Girl Scouts of the USA, as well as the president, Congress, AARP, corporate America, organized labor and cookie bakers across the country, those are minor hurdles.

I got a chance to put the plan into action when I dressed up as a giant Samoa cookie and helped Girl Scout Troop 2240 conduct a sale in Hauppauge, New York. My partners in this venture were Kaitlyn Lorenzen, Melanie Brusseler, Taylor Hogan, Dominique Napolitano and Josephine Waterman, all of whom are 11 years old, as well as Stephanie Verdone and Keri Smith, both 16, of Troop 1140. Sandra Napolitano, Dominique's mom, was the troop leader.

Kaitlyn was dressed in a Tagalong costume. The other girls wore their Scout uniforms. My outfit, a sleeveless smock with a large, smiling Samoa cookie face on the front, included a pair of the white, oversized, four-fingered gloves commonly worn by cartoon characters. If I had appeared in public like this when my daughters were Girl Scouts, they would have run away from home.

The girls and I set up shop in the H. Lee Dennison Building, where the Suffolk County offices are headquartered, and hoped to sell lots of cookies to visitors and county employees who came through on their lunch hour.

"If people are hungry, they'll buy more cookies," theorized Dominique, who has a bright future as a business tycoon.

There was just one problem: A grown man dressed as a Girl Scout cookie doesn't exactly inspire a feeling of safety.

"Wanna buy some cookies?" I asked as potential customers walked past. Most of them either didn't answer or, refusing to make eye contact with me, mumbled something about having already bought some.

Fortunately, the girls came to the rescue. They were far more persuasive (and a lot less threatening) than I was. Besides, they had a great marketing plan: Girl Scout cookies practically sell themselves.

One customer I didn't scare away, Beth Reynolds, who was a Girl Scout and is "proud of it," bought a dozen boxes, half of which she donated to Operation Cookie, which sends Girl Scout cookies to troops overseas.

"What do you think of my costume?" I asked.

"You look adorable," Reynolds replied.

When I asked her what she thought of my Social Security plan, she said, "I'd have to buy a lot more cookies, but it could work."

Deborah Weiner, a recent retiree, came up to me and said, "You're a cute cookie!" Then she bought a box of Reduced-Fat Lemon Coolers. When I asked Weiner about my Social Security idea, she said, "Anything can be a good idea." She paused and added, "Even yours."

Michelle Isabelle-Stark, whose two grown daughters were Girl Scouts, bought a box of Thin Mints from me. "It's as good a plan as anyone else has come up with," she said.

Even the girls thought I was on to something. Melanie spoke for them when she said, "It could help us save money for when we get to be your age."

At the end of my shift, I took off my Samoa costume and bought three boxes of cookies – one of Samoas, of course, and two of Do-si-dos, which are my favorites – and donated them to Operation Cookie.

"Awesome job!" Dominique said. "You were sweet – literally."

Melanie added, "You have a killer instinct. Ten thumbs way up!"

I thanked the girls, who were wonderful, and asked if they would have bailed me out if I had been arrested for selling cookies without a license.

"We like you," Kaitlyn said, "but that would have cut into our money."

As they say in the Girl Scouts, that's the way the cookie crumbles.

CHAPTER 8:
"FATHER OF THE BRIDE"

"Fully Engaged"

This wouldn't be good news to Spencer Tracy, who is dead and shouldn't care, or to Steve Martin, who is alive but doesn't know who the heck I am, but we all have something in common: I am going to be the father of the bride.

Katie just got engaged to her boyfriend, Dave. The wedding is set for November 3 in Boston. Sue and I are pleased and excited and abundantly proud to see such happiness in the eyes of a special young person who has our love and deserves nothing but the best.

We like Katie, too.

Dave's parents, Jane and Bob, who are wonderful people, feel the same way. They have raised a terrific young man who loves my daughter and treats her well and actually called me to ask for her hand. (No jokes about asking for the rest of her or I will come over to your house and hurt you.)

Naturally, the four parents (someday to be the four grandparents, who will shamelessly spoil Katie and Dave's children and then hand them back when it comes time to change diapers) have given our blessings to the union. In fact, we belong to Parents Union Local 123 (motto: "United we stand for everything except paying our kids' cell phone bills").

As the father of the bride, I have many important duties, the top two being: (a) renting a tuxedo and (b) letting the women take care of everything else.

The first will be more challenging because I haven't worn a tuxedo in almost 10 years, when I was the guest triangle player in a concert by the Stamford Symphony, which was conducted by the late Skitch Henderson (he was alive then, but he probably felt like dying when I introduced myself). I remember two things: I actually looked down in front of 1,500 people to make sure my fly wasn't open and, after miraculously not ruining the performance, I got a standing ovation.

I am hoping the same thing happens at the wedding.

My second duty will be much simpler because letting the women take care of everything else is what I do all the time anyway.

There is one thing, however, in which the women will have no part: the bachelor party. As the future father-in-law, I am sure I will have a prominent role and will no doubt have to contend with a key question: How about a stripper?

Answer: Forget it. I'm not taking my clothes off for anybody.

True, I will have a say in the guest list (I hope I'm invited) and in where the reception will be held. Sue and I have already seen a few places with Katie and Dave and have been wined and dined and haven't had to pay a penny. If only we could get the same deal for the wedding.

At one fancy joint, we were told we could have a choice of fish, chicken or steak. "What, no Happy Meals?" I inquired.

Sue, Katie and Dave reddened in embarrassment. I had another drink.

By November, I also will have to learn to dance. It probably would be easier to teach an orangutan, although it would be hard to tell us apart because we'd both be wearing monkey suits.

Speaking of which, Katie did me the honor of asking me to help her pick the song we will dance to. She doesn't know that my first choice for my own wedding song was "Three Blind Mice," which is the official Three Stooges theme, but for some strange reason Sue overruled me, so I picked Elvis Presley's "Can't Help Falling in Love," a slow tune that unfortunately prevented me from doing the Curly Shuffle out on the dance floor.

Still, Katie and Dave's wedding will be beautiful, a day filled with family and friends, lots of love and tears of joy.

And speaking of tears, there is one more question to answer: How am I going to pay for all this? That's easy.

If Hollywood can stand another remake of "Father of the Bride," I'm ready for my close-up.

"Meet the Zezimas"

When Katie and Lauren were young, they went through a period, roughly between kindergarten and college, in which they not only didn't want to be seen with me, they didn't want other people to know I even existed. I didn't take it personally because this happens to all parents, even Sue, who sometimes doesn't want to be seen with me herself.

But that is nothing compared to what happens when you are introduced to the parents of the person your son or daughter intends to marry. Sue and I were in this situation recently during our much-anticipated "Meet the Zezimas" weekend in Boston.

We had never met Jane and Bob, parents of Dave, fiancé of Katie, older daughter of Sue and Jerry, the aforementioned Zezimas, if you are scoring at home.

Sue and I, who had already met Dave and loved him, had spoken with Jane and Bob on the phone after Katie and Dave got engaged and found them to be very nice. But that was only an electronic, long-distance meeting. The ultimate challenge would be a face-to-face encounter.

The scene was a bar on a rainy Friday afternoon. Sue and I met Katie at work and walked to the downtown establishment, which I thought was the perfect meeting place, not only because it had a convivial atmosphere, but also because (and this was very important) it had an unlimited supply of alcohol.

We each ordered a glass of wine. Five minutes later, Dave and his parents walked in. Katie, who had already met her future in-laws, smiled at Sue and then looked at me. Her expression was like that of a deer caught in the headlights of a car. She seemed to be thinking: "Please, God, don't let him say anything stupid."

Dave walked up and kissed Katie. Then he kissed Sue, shook hands with me and introduced us to his folks. Jane hugged Sue and then me, after which Bob did the same. We hit it off instantly. Pretty soon we were chatting and laughing as if we had known each other for years. I could see Katie's abject fear begin to melt away, but there still were about 36 hours to go in the Great Parent Summit. Maybe, I could imagine her thinking, it wouldn't hurt if the old man came down with a sudden attack of laryngitis.

We all had dinner that evening in a terrific Chinese restaurant, where Bob and I decided to get down to the nitty-gritty and have a frank discussion about the subject that must be dealt with by men whose children are getting married. So we talked about baseball. The women chatted about shoes or something.

The next day, another rainy one, was extremely eventful. First, we all went on a Duck Tour aboard an amphibious vehicle from World War II that drove through downtown streets before converting to a boat that cruised the Charles River. Captain Johnny Baggadonitz allowed two boys, who were about 5 and 10 years old, respectively, to take the wheel. He did the same for a cute blonde who will be a college freshman in Boston this fall, when Katie and Dave will be married. I was going to ask if I could take command because I have captained every boat I have ever been on, including (this is absolutely true) a cruise ship. My sole qualification: I have a New York State driver's license.

But I thought better of it because with my luck, I'd hit a bridge or another boat and we would sink into the river, which would have ruined the wedding plans and put a real damper on the weekend.

Afterward, as the six of us stood in the lobby of a nearby hotel, Sue said to me, "We're splitting up."

"What?" I spluttered. "After 28 years of marriage? What message will this send to Katie and Dave?"

Sue rolled her eyes. "The women are going shopping," she said. "You men can go out for a beer."

Later, in a store, Jane reportedly said to Sue, "Jerry is very witty." To which both Sue and Katie responded, "We just ignore him."

After our respective excursions, we all went to the reception hall, which Jane and Bob had never seen, and then had dinner at a great Italian restaurant in the North End.

The weather may have been lousy all weekend, but the company was wonderful. Jane and Bob, who flew up from their home in South Carolina, are part of our family now. Sue and I, who drove up from our home on Long Island, couldn't be happier.

Neither could Katie and Dave because, against all odds, we didn't humiliate them. For all four parents, in the immortal words of Humphrey Bogart, this looks like the beginning of a beautiful friendship.

"Dancing With the Stiffs"

As a man with two left feet, which makes it extremely difficult to buy shoes, I have never been mistaken for Fred Astaire. Even in Astaire's present condition (dead), he is a better dancer than I am.

But with Katie's wedding coming up this fall, and not wanting to go out on the dance floor and act drunk, which creates a Catch-22 because I usually need a drink before I go out on the dance floor, I decided to take action. So Sue and I took a dancing lesson.

You can count on the toes of one foot the number of times we have been dancing in the past decade. That includes the wedding of the older son of our good friends Tim and Jane Lovelette, who had taken lessons in anticipation of the big day and were so good that they could have been on "Dancing With the Stars." Inspired by Tim and Jane's gracefulness, Sue and I got out on the dance floor and were just like Fred and Ginger – Fred Flintstone and Ginger from "Gilligan's Island."

That is why we went to the Arthur Murray Dance Studio in Port Jefferson Station, New York, to see if anyone, even the spirit of the late Arthur himself, could help us.

The first thing we found out from our instructor, Kevin, a very nice young man who is a theatrical dancer, as well as a tai chi and kung fu artist, is that Arthur Murray "wasn't a very good dancer."

"Does this mean I could have my own dance studio?" I asked.

"Why not?" said Kevin, who added that Murray was an excellent teacher and that his studios have been helping seemingly helpless cases for more than 90 years. "If you can walk through the door," Kevin said, "you can dance."

I had already made it through the door without mishap, so maybe there was hope for me yet.

But that didn't guarantee that I would not make a fool of myself. First, the studio was filled with people, young and old, who had come for dancing lessons, so I wouldn't be able to hide my incompetence. Second, because I was told to dress casually and bring dancing shoes, I wore an Old Navy T-shirt (with the cost of the wedding, I can't afford anything from New Navy), khaki shorts, white ankle socks and a pair of black wingtips. I looked like the biggest dweeb on the planet.

During the half-hour lesson, Kevin guided us through four basic dances: the foxtrot, the waltz, the rumba and the merengue. "These are called box dances because you go in a square," he explained.

"It's a good thing we're not going in a trapezoid or I'd be totally lost," I said.

We were already making progress because Sue and I usually dance in a circle, going around and around until we practically bore ourselves (and everyone watching) into the floor.

In addition to geometry, which I flunked in high school, I had to do basic math by counting to eight, over and over, to keep track of our steps: four moves, double the steps to account for each foot. "One, two, three, four, five, six, seven, eight," Kevin said, repeating himself like a broken record.

"This is why I can't balance the checkbook," I said.

Amazingly, Sue and I got the hang of it right away. And we didn't knock each other, or anyone else, over.

"This is fun!" Sue squealed.

It also was short. Before we knew it, the lesson was over. Kevin sat us down and gave us our grades. For balance and posture, Sue and I were "OK for now," Kevin said. Footwork: "Good." Leading and following: "Good." Animation and expression: "Good." Self-confidence: "Really good." Natural ability: "We need to work on that."

This meant, Kevin said, that Sue and I should sign up for a whole series of lessons. Unfortunately, the cost almost knocked me off my feet, which didn't even happen on the dance floor. Not that it would have bankrupted us, because under normal circumstances it was actually reasonable, but I had a choice: pay for dancing lessons or feed the wedding guests. I opted for the latter.

At least Sue and I won't humiliate ourselves at the reception. As long as we can channel the spirits of Fred and Ginger, not to mention a couple of spirits from the bar, it will be a step, or eight, in the right direction.

"Let Them Eat Cake"

Of the many things I have learned in the exciting and increasingly costly buildup to Katie's wedding, the most shamefully gluttonous one is that the person who coined the phrase "You can't have your cake and eat it, too" was never the father of the bride.

Not only can you have your cake, you can have eight slices of the richest, tastiest, most sinfully decadent desserts on earth and, at the risk of inflating to the size of the Goodyear blimp, eat them, too. For breakfast, no less.

That is what happened when Sue and I went with Katie and Dave to Konditor Meister, a renowned bakery in Braintree, Massachusetts, for a wedding cake tasting.

We had an appointment with Karen McCollem, a bridal consultant whose job is to consult the bride and help her select a cake that could, if necessary, feed the entire population of Luxembourg. In addition, she must see to it that the father of the bride suffers such a severe case of sugar shock that he won't keel over when presented with the bill for the big day.

"You should be a groomal consultant and a father-of-the-bridal consultant. We men don't know what the heck is going on," I told her.

Dave nodded. Karen smiled. "I'll add it to my resume," she said.

Karen, a witty and informal woman who insisted that we call her Karen (I was going to insist that she call me Mr. Zezima, but I didn't want to further humiliate Katie, though I eventually did anyway), sat us at an elegantly appointed table near a wall that was inscribed with the words, "Thou art a delicious torment."

"If you work here long enough, you'll probably get sick of cake," Dave said.

"Never," Karen replied. "And if we do, we just invent a new one." The latest, she said, was a mimosa cake filled with chocolate mousse, champagne and orange juice. Then she offered us coffee.

"I'll have a mimosa," I said.

"We don't have a license for that," Karen responded.

"You can always give them to us," Dave suggested.

We settled for water.

On the table was a large book containing dozens of photos of wedding cakes, including one that was topped with little figures of Marge and Homer Simpson in place of the traditional bride and groom.

"That one is pretty funny," Karen said. Katie and Dave nixed the idea.

"Speaking of funny, what do you think of using Three Stooges tactics?" I asked, referring to the practice in which the bride and groom are supposed to gently feed each other cake but instead mash it into one another's faces.

"It's absolutely unacceptable," Karen said firmly. "I bet a lot of people get divorced because of that."

"Nyuk, nyuk, nyuk," I noted.

Finally, it was time to pig out. Karen cut eight slices of cake and put them on the table for us to share. The selections were Apple Cinnamon Chai Torte, Tiramisu, Marble Torte, Raspberry Chambord Torte, Strawberry Grand Marnier, Cognac-Truffle Torte, Chocolate Torte and Carrot Torte. It was 11 a.m.

"There's nothing like cake for breakfast!" Sue exclaimed.

What followed was a feeding frenzy that would have given Miss Manners, not to mention anyone on a diet, a heart attack.

"What do you think of this one?" Katie asked as I shoved a hunk of Strawberry Grand Marnier into my mouth.

"Umph, umph, umph," I said approvingly.

At one point, Karen asked if we were going to have an alternate dessert. I said, "How about beer nuts?" Sue, Katie and Dave didn't even look up.

Needless to say, but I will say it anyway, because my mouth isn't full anymore, it was a great experience. I told Karen she was better than Martin Short, who played the bridal consultant in the remake of "Father of the Bride." She responded by saying, "Keck, keck, keck!"

Katie and Dave have pretty much decided what they want (some sort of chocolate and strawberry layer combination), with important input from Sue. As for me, it doesn't matter. When you're the father of the bride, this is the only part that is, to use another old saying, a piece of cake.

"Dad Takes a Bridal Shower"

Because I am a man, which doesn't say much for mankind, I never expected to be invited to a bridal shower. But because I am the father of the bride, and have been sweating Katie's upcoming wedding so much that I need a shower, I recently got a rare opportunity to attend one of these exclusive events, which not only featured other men, but was fueled by that most manly of beverages: beer.

That is what happened when Sue and I hosted a bridal shower for Katie. Not only did I get to go to the shower, which was held under a tent in our backyard, but Dave was there, too. The guest list included my father, my father-in-law and several of Katie and Dave's guy pals, including Mike, who figured prominently in the beer pong tournament that was held after many of the other guests had gone home.

Times sure have changed since Sue was a bride. In those days, bridal showers were for women only. Everyone wore dresses and the strongest drink was probably tea.

The men at Katie's shower drew the line at dresses and opted for pants, although I did wear a pink shirt. No tea was served. We did, however, have soda. And wine. And gin and vodka. And, of course, beer.

We stuck to tradition when Katie sat in a chair and opened her presents, prompting comments such as, "My goodness, that's a lovely serving plate," "Oh, what a beautiful cookie jar" and "What the heck is that?" The last remark was made, not surprisingly, by a guy.

Then came the moment of truth: Would the men have to provide the entertainment and put on a strip show like the kind made famous by the Chippendales dancers? Frankly, we men are tired of being treated as sex objects and wish that women would want us for our minds, which seldom happens because our minds are frequently clouded by beer. Besides, the thought of a bunch of flabby guys parading around in their boxer shorts was too much, not just for the women but also for Dave, who said to me, "If you want to do it, go right ahead." Not wishing to upset the guests, I wisely kept my pink shirt on.

Still, the shower was a smashing success, mainly because we men were on our best behavior, which means we didn't swear or belch (at least not too much) and the neighbors didn't have to call the cops. Some of us even made ourselves useful by tending bar for the ladies.

As the afternoon drew to a close, both my mother and my mother-in-law, who are veterans of traditional showers, said they had a blast. It was the supreme compliment.

Afterward, the remaining people, including Katie and Dave; Lauren, the maid of honor; and bridesmaids Amie and Ellen, all of whom stayed for the night, decided to extend the festivities. That's when Amie's husband, Mike, suggested beer pong. The idea of the game is to toss or bounce a ping-pong ball into one of several cups that are arranged at the opposite end of a long table. Each cup contains a small amount of beer. There are two players on each side. If an opposing player gets a ball into one of your cups, you or your teammate must drink the beer. This continues until either the cups or the players are gone.

As the tournament began, Dave and I added to the ambience by lighting up cigars. This may have been the first bridal shower in history to feature stogies.

Several games were played, including the championship contest pitting the bride and groom against the maid of honor and the father of the bride. I must say with all due modesty that, for a rookie, I played exceptionally well.

After a tense battle, Lauren and I emerged triumphant.

"I can't believe I played beer pong with Dad!" Lauren exulted.

"I can't believe he beat me!" Katie added.

I can't believe a bridal shower could be so much fun.

"Beautiful Schemer"

Since I always have my finger on the pulse (or at least in the nose) of fashion, I recently decided to give that finger, as well as the rest of my digits, some tender loving care. So I went to a spa for a manicure.

My day of beauty, which included a pedicure and a massage, was spent at Pro Nails in Setauket, New York. I treated myself because Katie is getting married, and she and Sue have been talking for weeks about how they are going to get all kinds of beauty treatments in preparation for the big day.

As the father of the bride, whose beauty treatment would have been limited to shaving and showering the morning of the wedding, I wanted to feel special, too.

The first thing I noticed was that, among the dozen or so customers and employees, I was the only man. The exception was Bruce, whose wife owns the place.

"My wife owns our place, too," I told Bruce. "She just lets me live there."

"I know what you mean," he said as he directed me to a large cushioned chair and instructed me to take off my shoes and socks and roll up my pants so I could stick my feet into a small tub that was filled with warm water. Then I was introduced to Yuki, a very nice aesthetician who must have felt like she was in "Mission: Impossible" because her mission, which she decided to accept, was to make me look beautiful.

She began by clicking a button that made the chair vibrate. Then she turned on a whirlpool in the tub and started rubbing my feet.

"My wife thinks I have the ugliest feet on earth," I told Yuki.

"You have very nice feet," she said with a smile. "Size 11, right?"

"How did you know?" I asked.

"You're tall," she replied while clipping my toenails. "If you were short, your feet would be too big. But they are just right."

I blushed. Other sensations flooded over me when Yuki slathered my feet and legs with a blue substance called body mud, which she slowly caressed into my calves. Then she covered my legs and feet with a clear plastic wrap like the kind used for leftover meatloaf. Or, as I noted, "feetloaf." After removing the wrap, Yuki buffed my heels and arches, which sent me into spasms of laughter. "You're ticklish," she said, giggling herself.

After anointing my feet with lotion, Yuki placed them on hot rocks, which made me feel like two orders of filet of sole. Then she washed everything off, dried me with hot towels, applied clear polish to my toenails, stuck small pieces of paper between my toes, put my feet into a pair of open-ended paper slippers, helped me out of the vibrating chair, and led me to a table for a manicure.

"You have very soft hands," Yuki remarked.

"That's because I don't do any real work," I explained.

As Yuki clipped my nails, she said, "You don't have any cuticles. That's very unusual."

"I have to tell you a secret," I confided. "I'm a Martian."

When she was finished soaking my fingertips and rubbing my hands, Yuki asked what color nail polish I wanted. "How about red?" she suggested.

"It would match my eyes," I replied, "but I don't want to compete with my wife's nails."

Yuki put on clear polish instead. Then she took me to a counter where my shiny fingernails and toenails were air-dried while she gave me a massage that was so heavenly, so wonderful, so absolutely fabulous that I was putty (and a fair amount of flab) in her hands.

When it was over, I put my socks and shoes back on, thanked Yuki for a great job and got compliments from the ladies. "You should do this once a month," one of them said. "You are so worth it," another one added. A third woman smiled and said, "You look beautiful."

For the father of the bride, it doesn't get any better than that.

"The Big Day"

When you're the father of the bride, you want your daughter's wedding to go off without a hitch. You also want it to go off with a hitch because otherwise your daughter wouldn't be married and essentially you will have spent all that money on a colossal hangover.

Happily, Katie did get hitched to Dave and, also happily, it all went off perfectly.

I don't like to brag, because I am a modest person not given to superlatives, most of the time with good reason, but this was the greatest wedding in the history of matrimony. Even in a post-reception fog, I can think of three good reasons:

1. Katie was a luminously beautiful bride.

2. Dave was a dashingly handsome groom.

3. I didn't fall on my face while walking Katie down the aisle.

Also, a great time was had by all. Sue, who was a beautiful mother of the bride, and I received unanimous raves, the most popular of which was: "You guys really know how to throw a party!"

Dave's parents, Jane and Bob, who are wonderful people with a terrific family, deserve a tip of the hat, too. That reminds me: Did I tip the bartender? God knows he deserved one.

Anyway, all of the preparation, all of the hard work, all of the stress leading up to the big day was well worth it, mainly because other people took care of everything. In my role as father of the bride, I was like a bobblehead doll: I nodded constantly. I also affixed my signature to so many dotted lines that I almost couldn't hold a fork at the reception. Then again, maybe it was because I was holding a drink.

The wedding, which was held at the Colonnade Hotel in Boston, the ideal venue because the staff made sure everything was perfect, took place on a Friday evening. As 6 o'clock approached and 105 people took their seats in the Boston Ballroom, I buttoned my tuxedo jacket and made sure my fly wasn't open. Then, as the music started and the bridesmaids and groomsmen began walking in, followed by Emma, the flower girl, I locked arms with Katie, kissed her, told her I loved her and said, "Here we go!"

Everything that followed was magical. I didn't trip, which was miraculous. I handed Katie off to Dave flawlessly. I acknowledged that I was the one giving away the bride without saying anything stupid. I watched and listened and, as Richard, the justice of the peace, pronounced Dave and Katie husband and wife, shed a tear. So did Sue.

When the doors opened at the reception in the main ballroom downstairs, it was like a Hollywood premiere. Sue and I were introduced and strutted in to the strains of Elton John's "I'm Still Standing." As a huge ovation washed over us, we felt like rock stars.

Then came the toasts. Adam, the best man, and Lauren, the maid of honor, were witty, touching and brief. By comparison, I gave a state of the union address. At one point, I said that Spencer Tracy and Steve Martin had nothing on me because no one has ever had more fun being father of the bride. Bob followed by saying that he was sure nobody could name the actors who have played the father of the groom.

At our table were my parents and Sue's parents. It was a blessing to see them enjoy their granddaughter's wedding. They even got down and boogied. Party animals!

Katie and I danced to Stevie Wonder's "You Are the Sunshine of My Life." That said it all. Sue and I danced to our wedding song, Elvis Presley's "Can't Help Falling in Love." After 28 years, it's still true.

Yes, it was a love fest, and a big party, and a celebration of life with family and friends, and a night to remember. And it all came off, beautifully and magically, both with and without a hitch.

CHAPTER 9:
"MISCELLANEOUS MUSINGS"

"Thanks for the Memory"

I'm a guy who often can't remember where he parked his car, which becomes a moot point if I don't know where I put my keys, so I was the last person who should have competed in a national brain-teasing event whose name unfortunately escapes me. Wait, now I remember: the USA Memory Championship, which was held amid much fanfare and media coverage at the ConEdison Building in New York City.

Actually, I wasn't the last person who should have competed because I did not, much to my shock, finish last. I can't recall exactly where I finished (I hope to locate the final standings before the end of this column), but let's just say that if I had any shame, I would have been humiliated.

Also, I was the only returning contestant from the inaugural USA Memory Championship 10 years ago and this time I was the oldest competitor (at 53, I am old enough to know better). That is not why I turned in such a pathetic performance, because many middle-age people have fantastic memories, except when it comes to finding their glasses, but I am not above making lame excuses.

As I parked my car in a garage a block from the event, I wondered whether I could possibly do any worse than I did in 1997, when I finished 14th in a field of 18. That included two contestants who didn't show up, probably because they forgot.

When I walked in, I was warmly greeted by Tony Dottino, a management consultant who founded the USA Memory Championship. He remembered me even after a decade because, he said, "You are not easy to forget."

With 41 contestants from across the country, the field had more than doubled since I last competed. Because the primary purpose of the USA Memory Championship is educational, there also were three high school teams whose members reminded me nothing of myself at that age, when the only things I could remember were baseball statistics and girls' phone numbers.

The organizers gave me a name badge that read: "Jerry Zezima, Mental Athlete." I'm no athlete, but they got the other part right.

In a futile effort to get inside the mind of one of my numerous mnemonic nemeses, I introduced myself to Dave Thomas (not the late founder of the Wendy's hamburger chain), a Britisher with dual citizenship: He lives in both Sandston, Virginia, and Yorkshire, England, from where he had flown for the event. Thomas, 38, is the author of "Essential Life Skills: Improving Your Memory." Since there was no way I could have read his book before the competition started (and even if I did, I'd never remember it all), I asked for his advice. Thomas answered, "Relax." Easy for him to say.

I sat down at a table with Paul Mellor, 48, a memory systems trainer from Richmond, Virginia. Most tables had two competitors, as well as a judge who administered a series of memory tests. Our judge was Colette Silvestri, a composer, playwright, lyricist, teacher and former legislative aide from Harrisburg, Pennsylvania. She asked if we had any questions. I said, "Can you be bribed?" She said, "No." I said, "Forget I ever mentioned it."

The first of the four qualifying events, which would narrow the field to seven finalists, was "Names and Faces," in which we had to memorize the names and faces of 99 people. I was so totally lost in the recall portion that under the photo of a guy with a beard, I wrote: "Grizzly Adams." Under the photo of a cute blonde, I wrote: "555-1234."

Still, I scored 13.5 points and was doing much better than I expected: I was only next-to-last. My standing didn't improve after the next event, "Speed Numbers," in which we had to memorize 25 rows of 40 numbers each. My score: 0.

I couldn't help but do better at "Speed Cards," in which we had to memorize the order of a shuffled deck of cards. For once in my life I was playing with a full deck. I didn't ace the event, but I did score 11 points.

I got 21 points in "Poetry," in which we had to memorize an unpublished poem, meaning I had gone from bad to verse. But it wasn't enough to put me in the finals. In fact, I finished a dismal 38th. The winner, not surprisingly, was Thomas, who will compete in the World Memory Championship in Bahrain. For me, it was a no-Bahrainer.

Still, I had such a good time at the USA Memory Championship that I plan to go back in another 10 years. My only other consolation is that I actually remembered where I parked my car.

"Amazing Braces"

I have fallen arches. This would be bad enough if they were in my feet, or even worse, if they fell while I was eating at McDonald's. But these arches are in my mouth, which is often stuffed with either Chicken McNuggets or one of my feet.

Actually, my maxillary arch is the site of a dental dilemma. So, in an effort to defeat this archenemy, I recently got braces.

My oral adventure began when I went to the Stony Brook University Dental Care Center on Long Island to see Dr. Ben Murray, an orthodontic resident who told me that while most of his patients are kids, some of them, like me, are baby boomers whose teeth have begun to wander. In this way, they are not discernibly different than my mind, except my teeth can be fixed.

Of my 28 pearly whites, 26 are straight. The other two, one on the top and the other on the bottom, are as crooked as some of the bigwigs on Wall Street. Unfortunately, my teeth don't qualify for federal bailout money.

Murray, a graduate of the University of Connecticut and the father of a baby boy who doesn't have teeth yet, told me I could get "invisible braces," which would not, I regret to inform family and friends, make my head disappear. But I know they work because Murray himself wears them and I couldn't tell. Then again, my eyes are in even worse shape than my teeth.

First, though, Murray and the Stony Brook staff had to review my case. Then I had to see Dr. Eugene Oh, an ace periodontist who gave me a series of "deep cleanings" that entailed freezing my face so I couldn't talk for most of the day. The aforementioned family and friends were very grateful.

Three weeks ago, I made an appointment with Janet Argentieri, an extremely nice orthodontic coordinator. "You'll see Dr. Murray next Wednesday at 10 a.m.," she said with a bright smile.

At the scheduled time, I was sitting in a reclining chair as Murray and certified orthodontic assistant Celeste DeGeorge peered into my big mouth, which resembles a cave but without the bats. All my bats are in the belfry.

I decided to get braces with ceramic brackets instead of the conventional metal ones, not just because they are more aesthetic, but because they match the cookware at home.

But these weren't the invisible braces I thought I was getting. Those, Murray said, would be applied in a year or so, after these braces do their job, which is to push back the tightly packed teeth in the upper right side of my mouth so there will be room for my lateral incisor to be rotated to its original position. The invisible braces will then be applied to both my top and bottom teeth. A year after that, Murray promised, I'll have the smile of a Hollywood star. I assume he wasn't referring to Freddy Krueger.

"For now," Murray said, "we're working on the right buccal segment of the maxillary arch to distalize that area and correct the Class 2 malocclusion."

"You took the words right out of my mouth," I replied.

What Murray put into my mouth was a track resembling a stretch of the Long Island Rail Road. It was a construction project that, I was relieved to find out, would not involve either jackhammers or dynamite.

"But we will have to use a blowtorch," Murray announced, adding that the flame would be applied to a wire not already in my mouth.

"You have very shiny teeth!" DeGeorge exclaimed. "What do you use on them?"

"Turtle Wax," I told her.

The procedure lasted less than an hour. It didn't hurt at all, even without Novocaine, and the braces, which begin on my second molar, are mostly hidden by my cheek. This means I won't be the star of a TV show called "Ugly Jerry."

I can't chew gum (especially while walking) and I have to avoid such hard or sticky foods as peanut brittle, caramel and pizza crust. But I can still eat Chicken McNuggets to my heart's content. And I don't have to worry about fallen arches.

"The Eyes Have It"

I have always viewed myself as a farsighted person, a visionary who, like a great leader, could clearly see the world around me. After a visit to the eye doctor, however, I know I'm a nearsighted person, a double-visionary who, like Mr. Magoo, can't see much past my nose.

Fortunately, my nose isn't my most delicate feature, so I'm not totally blind to the world around me.

That's how Dr. Howard Weinberg saw me when I went to see him.

I recently walked into Eyecare Unlimited in Coram, New York, humming Jackson Browne's "Doctor, My Eyes" because I hadn't gone to an eye doctor since the Clinton administration, which is what I put on the paperwork I had to fill out.

Weinberg, an optometrist who also is an optimist, looked at the form through a pair of stylish glasses and asked, "Why did you wait so long to get your eyes examined? A change of administrations?"

"It's going on two administrations," I pointed out. I also thought I heard him humming "Jeepers Creepers, Where'd You Get Those Peepers?"

It must have been what he was thinking when he peered into my orbs through a machine that looked, at least to the untrained eye, like a small version of the Hubble Space Telescope.

Then Weinberg asked me to look at the chart on the wall.

"What wall?" I said.

He ignored the remark and told me to read the first three lines. They were:

E

FP

TOZ

"Very good," he said. "Now read the next three."

They weren't so easy. Here's what I thought I saw:

YOU

CANTSEE

HAHAHAHA

"You're myopic and you have a touch of astigmatism," Weinberg said. "Do you wear glasses?"

"Yes, but only for driving," I said, handing him the pair I got a decade and a half ago. "They're bent, so they make my head look lopsided," I added.

"Maybe it's not the glasses," Weinberg replied with a smile. Then he explained that with my prescription, a 9-by-9 room will appear to be 9-by-12.

"You mean my house is bigger than I thought?" I asked.

Weinberg nodded. "Good news in a bad market," he said. "Maybe I should go into real estate."

Then he gave me a glaucoma test, which entailed using drops that dilated my pupils. While waiting for the solution to take effect, I thought of the Three Stooges and how Moe would poke his fingers into the eyes of Larry, Curly and, depending on the episode, Shemp.

"If they were my patients," Weinberg said, "I'd make a fortune."

Keeping with the musical theme, Crystal Gayle's "Don't It Make My Brown Eyes Blue" started playing in my head, except the drops made them red, which is their primary color.

"You don't have glaucoma," Weinberg said, adding that I have 20/40 vision. "That's not bad," he said. "You can keep the same prescription, but you might want to get more stylish glasses."

Weinberg's wife, Jill, the smartly bespectacled office manager, helped fit me for a new pair. "I'd go with a more rectangular look," she suggested. "You have nice eyes. They're very large."

"Like Barney Google's?" I said.

"And you have an oval face," the good doctor noted.

"You mean I'm an egghead?"

The Weinbergs, a terrific couple with excellent senses of humor, chuckled and assured me that I'd look even better with "more modern" glasses. Because I'm a mild-mannered reporter for a great metropolitan newspaper, I chose a pair that will help keep my secret identity and might even put me on the cover of GQ.

"Now, when you drive," Jill said, "you'll not only be able to see traffic lights and stop signs, but you'll look good to other drivers."

As I left the office, I glanced in the mirror and hummed "I Only Have Eyes for You."

"Out of Shape and Into Yoga"

As a dedicated couch potato who would eat potatoes on the couch if Sue would let me, I firmly believe that exercise can kill you. After decades of being ridiculously sedentary, I still have not only my boyish figure but also, if barely, a heartbeat.

Lately, however, I have begun to think that I really ought to do more than what is now my main form of physical activity: 12-ounce curls.

So I recently took a yoga class.

I signed up for one very important reason: It was free. And, all modesty aside, I figured I was worth every penny.

Also, I received great encouragement from Katie, who is something of a yoga guru. She has been taking classes for the past few years and once participated in a "yoga challenge," which required participants to do yoga every day for a month. I would have been dead on Day Three.

"Are you doing hot yoga or regular yoga?" Katie asked.

"What's the difference?" I replied.

"About 40 degrees," Katie said, explaining that regular yoga takes place at room temperature, whereas hot yoga is done at 110 degrees. At that rate, I'd have to be in either a sauna or Death Valley, so I was guessing – and hoping – it was the regular kind.

Then Katie said that I had to buy a yoga mat.

"What's that?" I inquired.

"It's a mat," Katie said, very patiently, "on which you do yoga."

Who would have guessed? So I forked over $12 for a baby blue mat that perfectly matched the baby blue T-shirt I planned to wear to the class. After all, it's nice to be fashionable, especially when you're sweating like a stuck pig.

The first thing I noticed about the yoga class, which was held at work, was that there were 20 women and one guy. That guy was, of course, yours truly.

"Is this your first time?" asked Diane, who took a spot behind me.

"Yes," I said bashfully as I unfurled my yoga mat. Then I asked if anyone knew CPR, which I figured I would need, although I was worried that my T-shirt would blend in with my mat and nobody would notice that I had collapsed.

"You'll do fine," Liz, another participant, said reassuringly.

I hoped I could say the same for the women around me because the instructor, Dawn, suggested that we do the session in bare feet. Fortunately, when I removed my sneakers and socks, nobody keeled over.

Dawn began the class by talking about positions, none of which was third base or, the place where I am always accused of being, left field. Instead, she said we would be doing down dog, plank, cobra and warrior 2. They involved gently stretching, twisting and otherwise contorting our bodies in ways I didn't know a body could move. I must have looked like a cloverleaf on the interstate highway system.

Dawn instructed us to extend one arm while crossing the opposing leg over our bodies as we lay on our yoga mats. Then we had to get on all fours and extend one leg, then the other. I was so confused that I resorted to cheating by looking at the other participants to see which limb I was supposed to be lifting, extending or stretching at any given moment.

At the end of the 45-minute class, I had a sense of both peace (the soothing music helped) and accomplishment (because I didn't have to be hospitalized). In fact, I have seldom felt better.

"You did very well," Dawn told me afterward. When I said I hadn't exercised in years, she said, "You look like you're in really good shape."

"Looks can be deceiving," I noted, "but this made me feel great. I'm not sore at all."

"That's because we did hatha yoga," Dawn explained.

"Well," I replied, "hatha yoga is better than none."

Dawn politely ignored the remark and said that hatha is the regular kind of yoga, while Bikram is the hot version.

Either way, I had such an enjoyable experience that I would definitely take another class. Until then, maybe I can be a couch potato on my yoga mat.

"Web of Intrigue"

Itsy-bitsy spider crawled up the shower head, and gave me such a huge fright I almost dropped dead.

This tune has been playing over and over in what little remains of my mind since I had a terrifying encounter with a spider the other morning and somehow lived to tell about it.

I am a man who loves God's creatures, even most members of Congress, but I must admit that I am not crazy about spiders. And the one I saw in the shower was the biggest, meanest, most frightening beast in the history of bugdom.

Yes, I know that spiders are not technically bugs, or insects, but are arachnids (a scientific word meaning "they who give you the willies and can kill you with one bite") and are closely related, on their father's side, to wolves.

This one must have been a second cousin of Lon Chaney Jr., only hairier, because I could have sworn (and did, several times) that it howled at me, although it could have been either the rushing water or the pounding of my heart, which almost stopped when I saw the monster.

My first instinct was to kill him. That's exactly what I had done the night before, when I squashed his brother in the kitchen. Of course, it may not have been his brother. It could have been his brother-in-law, or a neighbor he never really liked, or even someone he met in a chat room on the Web. Or maybe the spider in the shower wasn't a guy. It could have been a female, and the one I killed the night before could have been her husband, which would have made her a ... *black widow!*

Now I was really scared. I was going to pulverize the thing with a shampoo bottle when it darted around back of the other shampoo bottles on the rack hanging from the shower head and disappeared. I moved against the wall and conjured images from "The Incredible Shrinking Man," the 1957 science-fiction classic in which a man who has shrunk to the size of an ant has a mortal showdown with a spider that, compared to him, is as big as a Volkswagen.

Then I said to myself, "Calm down, you fool. This spider is probably more scared of you than you are of it." I began to think warm thoughts about the species, especially about Charlotte, the charming heroine of "Charlotte's Web," and for a moment I could imagine my spider companion weaving loving messages to me. I looked through the rushing water and thought I saw a web. I looked harder. There was a message. It read: "DEAD MAN WASHING."

By this time, I was in a panic. What was I going to do, run naked into the street, screaming about the spider in the shower? The neighbors would have locked their doors and called the cops. Then the men in the white coats would have come and taken me away in a butterfly net. I thought it over for a long time, as the water bill increased to the point where it rivaled my life savings, because at least butterflies can't kill you.

In the worst-case scenario, I imagined I was bitten by the spider and had to be rushed to the hospital, where I had the following exchange with the attending physician.

Doctor: "It's pretty small."

Me: "Listen, doc, I didn't come here to be insulted!"

Doctor: "No, I mean the bite."

Me: "Oh."

In the end (another place I could imagine being bitten), the spider and I reached an uneasy truce. I finished my shower unharmed and he, most likely, took a powder.

The only good thing to come out of the encounter is that I am now saving water by taking faster showers. And, for what it's worth, I have the cleanest spider in the neighborhood.

"Shark Dive"

One of the scariest things about the movie "Jaws," the heartwarming tale of a great white shark who loved people so much he just ate them up, was the music. Playing ominously in the background was John Williams's Oscar-winning score, which went like this: "Dumb-dumb-dumb-dumb, dumb-dumb-dumb-dumb."

That described me when I went to Atlantis Marine World Aquarium in Riverhead, New York, for what I feared would be a once-in-a-lifetime experience called a Shark Dive.

Instead of encountering a great white, or even a mediocre white, I came face-to-face with nine sharks that had a combined total of what appeared to be several million teeth, each of which could sever a major artery, such as Interstate 95 or the Long Island Expressway. Six were sand tiger sharks, the largest of which measured 7 feet long, weighed 300 pounds and was named Bertha, and three were nurse sharks, in case Bertha was hungry and I needed medical care. Unfortunately, there were no doctor sharks, but there was a gigantic loggerhead turtle that weighed more than Bertha and was named – this was the really scary part – Jaws.

The Shark Dive took place in the aquarium's 12-foot-deep, 120,000-gallon tank, which also is home to lots of other creatures, including a stingray and a moray eel, neither of which is mentioned in my life-insurance policy.

Speaking of which, I had to sign a waiver absolving Atlantis Marine World and, though not mentioned specifically by name, Bertha from any blame in case I needed the services of the Davy Jones Funeral Home ("For all of your at-sea burial needs").

I should point out that I was in a metal cage that provided protection against the tank's most dangerous creature: me. It seems sharks are in more danger from humans than the other way around, probably because the most frightening sharks are called – you guessed it – lawyers.

"We hear a lot of lawyer jokes," said marine biologist Chris Paparo, who with Kate Hanson, the aquarium's head shark dive educator, told me everything I wanted to know about sharks but was afraid to ask. For example, sharks can smell one drop of blood from a mile away. They also can detect the heartbeat of a potential meal.

"Don't worry," Hanson assured me, "sand tiger sharks eat only fish and other long, soft-bodied creatures."

"Wait a minute," I said as my heartbeat picked up. "I'm a long, soft-bodied creature."

I thought I was nervous until I met Anthony Esposito, who would be going on the Shark Dive with me. Esposito's wife, Idina, had given him the dive, which costs $155, for his 39th birthday. She and their children, Anthony Jr., 13, Brendan, 10, and Giulia, 8 months, were there to watch and, because you never know what might happen, kiss him goodbye.

Even though Esposito is a trainer for Brazilian jujitsu welterweight champion Matt Serra, requiring him to spar with Serra in a cage, which to me would be worse than being in a shark cage, he admitted: "I'm scared."

There really was no reason to be. Dive master Ken LaPeters, who would be in the cage with us, made sure we were thoroughly schooled in what to do, from donning our wet suits to putting on our masks, which had microphones so we could talk with each other. The masks also were hooked up to air tanks, which made me breathe a lot easier.

LaPeters's son, Ken Jr., 10, who said he wants to be like his dad when he grows up, helped me on with my rubber shoes. "Have fun!" he said before the three of us were locked in the cage and lowered into the tank.

Fun was an understatement. For half an hour, I had the most exhilarating and educational experience of my life. I chatted away with LaPeters, who is funny, dedicated and knowledgeable; gave the thumbs-up sign to the visibly less nervous Esposito, who waved as his wife and kids took pictures from outside the glass tank; and said hello to Bertha, who swam by several times, as did the other sharks, but apparently – and fortunately – found me extremely unappetizing.

I now have a greater appreciation for sharks and other undersea life, which is the point of the Shark Dive. And, unlike a lot of people in "Jaws," I lived to tell about it.

"Show Me the Money"

In these challenging economic times, when a middle-class guy like myself can't get a federal bailout or an AIG bonus, even though my tax dollars are helping to pay for it all, it's nice to know that there are some people who are willing to give me lots of money.

I refer to the kind folks who have been sending me e-mails from all over the world with an offer I can't, they hope, refuse: In exchange for my assistance in transferring huge sums of cash to the United States, which would entail giving them vital personal information, these generous individuals will give me a significant percentage of the millions of dollars in their foreign bank accounts.

They include Dr. Bakary Sawadogo of Ouagadougou, Burkina Faso, Africa; Mr. Zuma Camara, who is from Liberia but now lives in the United Arab Emirates; Mr. Egor Fillipenko, who works for a large oil company in Moscow, Russia; Sgt. Joey Jones, who is stationed with the U.S. Army in Iraq; Mr. Ken Ahia, an attorney representing a late relative of mine somewhere in the Middle East; and Miss Jessica Yao, a desperate young woman who lives in the Republic of Cote d'Ivoire, formerly known as the Ivory Coast in West Africa.

To all of these people I responded with the following message: "Show me the money."

You can imagine my surprise and delight when I actually heard back from some of them. Here is the reply I got from Mr. Ahia:

"Dear Zezima,

"I am Barrister Ken Ahia, a solicitor at law. I am the personal attorney to the late Mr. Ali Zezima, who bears the same last name with you, a national of your country.

"See my attached message.

"Best regards,

"Barrister Ken Ahia"

Naturally, the attached message contained a plea to help Mr. Ahia transfer a large sum of money to the United States through my bank account. Here is my reply:

"Dear Barrister Ahia:

"Cousin Ali is dead? I am desolated beyond words at this terrible news! Is it true he died in a tragic bungee jumping accident? Or that he was bitten in a sensitive area by a poisonous spider? Or that he was caught in flagrante delicto (Flagrante Delicto is a popular resort where cousin Ali often went to escape his legal troubles) by the husband of the wealthy woman with whom he was having a torrid affair?

"Please write back to fill me in on the scandalous details and to arrange to send all of his money to my bank account here in the United States.

"Best regards,

"Jerry Zezima"

Strangely, I have not had further contact with Mr. Ahia. But I did hear from Miss Jessica Yao, an orphaned college student who has been targeted for murder by the thugs who killed her father, a wealthy cocoa merchant. They want to get their bloody hands on her father's fortune, which is why she wishes to transfer the money, through me, to the United States. Miss Yao wrote to me, in part, as follows:

"My Dear,

"Thanks for your prompt responds and my heartily greetings to you this day. I am glad for your interest in helping me with the funds transfer and investments in your country. Please promise me that you will not betray me when my inheritance is transferred into your account. ... God bless you.

"Best wishes with love,

"Yours sincerely,

"Miss Jessica Yao"

Here is my reply:

"Dearest Jessica:

"It grieves me to read of your troubles, which have touched my heart. I was already touched in the head. You probably think I am an easy touch, which is why you have written to me.

"I am a newspaper columnist who had to take a vow of poverty when I went into journalism, so I could use the money. Your story will be of great interest to readers around the world, including, I am sure, the authorities.

"Please respond quickly, dear one, for I desire to transact with you. It will be chaste, unless you are chased, by the police, who may want to arrest you for fraud, in which case I will have the funds to bail you out. At the very least, I'll send you a postcard from the new vacation home your money will enable me to buy. God bless you.

"Best wishes with love,

"Yours sincerely,

"Jerry Zezima"

Unfortunately, I have not had further correspondence with Miss Yao or any of the other nice people who wanted to make me rich. But I am not giving up. Maybe, with the help of our elected officials, I can get some money from AIG.

"Jailhouse Talk"

As a columnist whose work has no redeeming social value, which has no doubt contributed to the decline of the newspaper industry, I knew it was only a matter of time before my journalistic crimes landed me in jail. I just didn't think I would end up on Rikers Island.

But New York City's famous maximum-security prison is exactly where I found myself recently after I was asked by a teacher – not sentenced by a judge – to spend a day at the facility. The purpose of my visit was to address three writing classes at Horizon Academy, a school for detainees in their teens and 20s.

When I asked the teacher, Martin Flaster, how to get to Rikers Island, he said, "Rob a bank." Of course, a bank is the last place to go for money these days, but I knew I was in for a memorable time.

Mary Runyan, a secretary at Horizon Academy, picked me up at the guard post and drove me over the Francis R. Bruno Memorial Bridge (the word "memorial" made me nervous) to the 400-acre site, which sits in the East River near LaGuardia Airport.

"I feel safer here than I would at a regular high school," Runyan said.

"Why?" I asked.

"Because," she replied calmly, "there are no guns here."

That made me feel better, and although Runyan didn't mention knives, shivs, blades or other dangerous weapons, I was sure the inmates had more to fear from me, at least psychologically, than I did from them. I figured a day of listening to me talk about writing would have most of them begging for solitary confinement.

It was only when I was escorted in and heard a barred door lock behind me that I thought: "Uh-oh."

As it turned out, I could not have felt more welcome or comfortable. Gloria Ortiz, principal of Horizon Academy, and her entire staff, including Flaster and senior program specialist Cherie Braxton, were wonderful. So were the guards. The inmates I passed in the halls were respectful. Some even said, "Good morning." Others just ignored me. So, unfortunately, do most people on the outside.

I am not some bleeding heart (I hate the sight of my own blood), so I believe that if you do the crime, you should do the time. And the crimes here can be pretty serious. Let me put it this way: Nobody goes to Rikers Island for jaywalking.

But the young men in Horizon Academy, which has about 300 students in six buildings, haven't been convicted of anything. True, they have been charged with various offenses and most of them are awaiting trial. And even though they are officially called detainees, they get locked up like all the other inmates. But they are in school, some to improve their literacy skills and others to get their general equivalency diplomas.

I met the first class at 11 a.m. in the school annex. The group was so large (36 students) that it had to be held in a hallway, where desks were lined up against both walls. This didn't bother me because I'm off the wall, so instead of standing at one end, I walked among the students and talked about different kinds of writing. A student named Emerson asked if I could write a rap song.

"Well," I said, "my initials are J.Z., which makes me a rapper."

"Let's hear one," said Urena, another student.

I happily obliged: "My name's J.Z. and I love to rap. / Unfortunately, I sound like crap."

It was politely suggested that I shouldn't quit my day job.

Then I read one of three columns I had sent to the school before my visit. It was a recent piece in the form of a letter to President Barack Obama, from one family man to another, giving the new commander-in-chief advice on moving into the White House and what to do when he gets his two young daughters the puppy he promised them.

The students applauded when I finished, and not because they were glad it was over. I felt good about the session, but the other two went more smoothly because they were smaller and were held in classrooms.

Teacher John Parada's English class had eight students: Danny, Cary, Adam, Kenny, Donovan, Travis, Martinez and Anonymous. They were engaging, sharp and interested in writing. They also had good senses of humor.

"How do you know when to use a colon?" asked Travis, setting me up for a bathroom joke.

When I read my Obama column, which contained the story of the time I called the White House to see if then-President George W.

Bush would declare my younger daughter's room a federal disaster area, Adam asked, "Did you really call Bush?"

"Yes," I told him.

"Man," Adam said, smiling and shaking his head, "you're crazy."

"Thank you," I replied. "I was dropped on my head as a child."

Cary said I was "cool," adding: "For your age."

The class was fun – we talked about humor, fiction, nonfiction, language and editing – and went by quickly. When it was over, Martinez, a poet, asked if he could send me some of his work. "Of course," I said. I hope he does.

After a late lunch in another building, I spoke to the third group, Martin Flaster's English class, which consisted of Eduardo, Lil Haye, Strictly 50, Lorenzo, Fever, HOV, James, B.B., Naquan and Leon, who used to live in my hometown of Stamford. Teacher and site coordinator Leila Riley helped Flaster conduct the class.

These students also were sharp and engaging. And creative: Instead of listening to me read my column, Eduardo, also known as "A-Rod," suggested that each student read a paragraph out loud. Around the room went the column, provoking laughs, chuckles and smiles.

"Good job," Eduardo said to his classmates when they were finished.

Lorenzo said to me, "You did a good job, too." The class laughed. Then he read an essay he had written. It was a letter to a young woman that Lorenzo said "could be" autobiographical. It was eloquent and touching.

James and Leon talked about books that are made into movies, with Leon saying that the film adaptations usually aren't as good as the books because "a lot of stuff has to be left out."

At one point, James politely criticized my word choice when, in explaining the differences between writing and other professions, I said that airplane pilots need degrees to fly. "That's wrong," James noted. "They need certificates."

"I stand corrected," I said.

"You mean you sit corrected," Lorenzo remarked. More laughter.

At the end of the class, Eduardo said to me, "You were really good because you were honest with us."

Flaster said the students would write essays about the session and send them to me. Then he asked if I would keep in touch. "Yes," I promised.

As I told the guys in each of the three classes, "potential" is one of the most overused words in the English language, but it applies to them because they all have it. I said they should use it in a positive way so they can improve their lives, adding: "If an idiot like me can make it, there's hope for you."

To the charge of enjoying my day in prison, I plead guilty. Since the staff of Horizon Academy didn't consider me a bad influence on the students, and the students seemed to agree, I would definitely go back. And I wouldn't even have to rob a bank.

"Fast Paul and the Ping-Pong Kid"

Paul Newman had such a delightfully wry and self-deprecating sense of humor that he probably wouldn't mind if I said I'm glad I'm not the reason he's dead. But I came close to killing him several years ago, when the legendary actor and popcorn pooh-bah almost choked on a bowl of Zezima's Zesty Ziti Zinger.

The first ingredient in my recipe for near-disaster was a ping-pong ball, which came into play when someone from the office of Newman's Own, the Westport, Connecticut-based food company that sells salad dressing and gives lots of lettuce to charity, called to ask if I wanted to play Fast Paul in a game of table tennis at the Rainbow Room in New York City.

I immediately accepted the challenge because the game would be played at the awards luncheon for the annual Newman's Own and Good Housekeeping Recipe Contest and, being a serious journalist, I knew there would be free eats.

The place was filled with more than 100 people, not just contest winners from across the country but celebrities such as Regis Philbin, Kathie Lee Gifford and writer A.E. Hotchner, Newman's Westport neighbor and his partner in the food company. And right in the middle was the ping-pong table, at one end of which stood Newman, paddle in hand. I was at the other end. A woman from Newman's Own wore a striped shirt and carried a whistle. She was the referee.

I quickly learned one thing about Paul Newman: His propensity for cheating was, I am sorry to say, even greater than mine.

He hit a shot into the net. The ref said, "Point, Mr. Newman."

I hit a forehand smash past the athletic star. "Point, Mr. Newman."

One of his shots was long. "Point, Mr. Newman."

It continued in this fashion until I was utterly defeated.

The crowd roared. Newman shook my hand and said, "Nice game, kid."

At least he fed me.

Being not just a glutton for punishment but a glutton, period, I went back for more the next year. But the luncheon was delayed because there was a fire in the kitchen at the Rainbow Room. By the time it was out, the entertainment portion of the program had to be shelved.

"Is it true that you used some of your hot sauce to start the fire so you could weasel out of playing me in a rematch?" I asked Newman.

He winked one impossibly blue eye and replied, "You might want to say that."

The following year, I created a dish and brought it to the luncheon for Newman to try. The ingredients were garlic, onions, chicken, hot sausage, red and green peppers, salt, black pepper, red pepper and a jar each of Newman's Own Bombolina and Sockarooni sauces. I also poured in some red wine and vodka and served the whole thing over a bed of pasta.

I fed the concoction, which I dubbed Zezima's Zesty Ziti Zinger, to my family. Miraculously, nobody had to be hospitalized, so I put some in Sue's best Corningware dish and brought it to the luncheon.

For some reason or other, Newman never got a chance to try it. To make matters worse, the Corningware dish got misplaced and was never found. To this day, Sue has not forgiven me. But Waldy Malouf, executive chef of the Rainbow Room, sampled my creation and said it was delicious. "You should enter it in next year's contest," he suggested.

So I did. I filled out the entry form with my recipe and mailed it in. A few weeks later, I got a phone call informing me that I was the runner-up in the pasta sauce division. I, a man who can barely make toast, had finished second in a field of thousands.

I made another batch and fed some to my dog, Lizzie, just to make sure it was OK. Lizzie wolfed it down and wanted more, but I put the remainder in a Tupperware container – no Corningware this time – and brought it to the awards luncheon.

Afterward, I went up to Newman with my plastic bowl of Zezima's Zesty Ziti Zinger and asked if he wanted to try it. "Sure, kid," he said, grabbing a fork.

As he was shoveling in the first mouthful, I told him I had fed some to my dog and that if it was good enough for her, it would be good enough for him, too.

"Gack!" Newman said in mid-chew. Then his eyes bulged, his face flushed and he gasped for air.

"Oh, God!" I thought. "He's going to choke to death on my recipe. I'll forever be known as the man who killed Paul Newman."

Fortunately, he recovered, swallowed the mouthful and asked, "Is your dog still alive?"

"Yes," I assured him.

That was all Newman needed to hear. He scarfed down the rest of the Zinger, saying between bites, "Mmmm! This is – umph, umph, umph – delicious! You could have been a winner, kid."

Thanks to the man with a great appetite for life and a twinkle in those famous eyes, I sure felt like one.

Point, Mr. Newman.

"A Work of Art"

Art Buchwald was the reason I became a writer. But please don't blame him. Fault for the many journalistic crimes I have committed over the past 31 years is entirely mine.

There have been many positive influences in my life, but only two men have really been heroes to me. My father, who will be 90 in October and is still going strong, is my personal hero. Buchwald, who died recently at 81, was my professional hero.

When I was a student at Stamford Catholic High School in the early 1970s, Buchwald spoke at an assembly in the auditorium. He was hilarious. I didn't meet him, but after his speech, I began to read his column in The Stamford Advocate. He was as funny in print as he was in person.

"That," I remember saying to myself, "is what I want to do. I want to be like Art Buchwald."

In 1976, a year out of college, I got a job as a copy boy at The Advocate. It took me nine years, eight as a sportswriter and one as a city editor, to achieve my goal of being a humor columnist.

At first, I was a shameless Buchwald imitator (Robert Benchley and Erma Bombeck also were great influences), but gradually I developed my own style. It paled next to Buchwald's. It still does. But all these years I have done something I love, if only because I am spectacularly unqualified to do anything else.

In 2002, I did something I never could work up the nerve to do before: I wrote Buchwald a letter, telling him that he was why I got into journalism and thanking him for the fact that I was in a field that not only didn't require me to do any real work, but which paid so little money that it actually simplified my tax returns. To my great surprise and delight, he wrote back. It was a nice, cheery, funny letter.

Over the past five years, we exchanged letters and chatted on the phone. I found Buchwald to be just as nice and just as funny as I hoped he would be. I was proud and happy to nominate him for the Ernie Pyle Lifetime Achievement Award from the National Society of Newspaper Columnists, which Suzette Martinez Standring, then president of the NSNC, presented to him in a hospice last February.

After being diagnosed with terminal kidney failure and having a leg amputated because of circulatory problems, Buchwald declined further dialysis and checked into the hospice in Washington, D.C., to live out what doctors said would be his final two or three weeks.

Fittingly, the King of Humor had the last laugh: He hung on far longer than anyone thought he would. He held court at the hospice; he regaled visitors with funny stories; he wrote in a column that he was being called "The Man Who Wouldn't Die"; he said in a TV interview that he was "hearing from girlfriends I didn't even know I had"; and he gorged on McDonald's hamburgers and milkshakes.

After leaving the hospice, he wrote the last of his 35 books, "Too Soon to Say Goodbye." It is one of his best.

In 2005, I wrote a rare political column (I usually write about things that have no redeeming social value) and sent it to Buchwald. Here was his reply:

"Dear Jerry,

"Thank you so much for sending me the article. I enjoyed it very much, and if you write any more political ones, I'll have one of my guys break your legs.

"Cheers,

"Art Buchwald"

A month later, I pushed my luck and wrote another political column. I also had been a small help (the only kind I could ever be) in arranging for Buchwald to speak at a fundraiser for Standring's hometown library in Milton, Massachusetts. The event was held at the John F. Kennedy Library in Boston. And, although I have absolutely no influence, even in my own home, I had asked a couple of editor friends of mine whether they would once again run Buchwald's column, which over the past few years had been dropped by some papers. It was the least I could do for the man who meant so much to me. All of this prompted Buchwald to write:

"Dear Jerry,

"Thanks for your letter and for the column. My boys are making cement shoes for you as you read this.

"Thanks for going to bat for me with the Stamford and Newsday papers. It's rare that one columnist would push another columnist, and I'm grateful.

"I had a wonderful time in Boston. I sat next to Suzette at dinner and we had fun. The two of you are my biggest boosters and I love you both.

"Cheers,

"Art"

I loved Art Buchwald, too. He was one of the most influential newspaper columnists of the past half-century and one of the greatest humorists in the history of American journalism. He also was a good guy. And one of my heroes.

CHAPTER 10:
"SUE & JERRY'S EXCELLENT ADVENTURES"

"Love and Marriage"

Now that Sue and I have been married for 30 years, family and friends have suggested that for putting up with me for so long, she deserves to be the first living person canonized by the Catholic Church. I, they add, deserve to be shot from a cannon.

What is the secret of our long and happy marriage? The answer, according to researchers at the University of Michigan, is that we get on each other's nerves.

In a recent study, the researchers found that as a couple ages, a lifetime of closeness rubs up a rash of irritations. Participants in the study, which was presented at the Gerontological Society of America, were asked who in their lives – spouse, children or friends – "gets on my nerves" or "makes too many demands on me." The older the couple, the more likely the answer was "spouse."

But, strangely enough, rubbing each other the wrong way may be the right way to conduct a marriage. One of the reasons that couples quarrel is that they are closer and more comfortable with each other. As we age, the researchers concluded, "it could be that we're more able to express ourselves to each other."

Sue and I seldom quarrel, not only because I know I will lose but because I am almost always wrong. Even Sue will concede that I am right about this.

Nonetheless, I risked getting on her nerves by conducting my own study on our 30th anniversary.

Being a couple of real swingers, Sue and I celebrated by going out to lunch. Of course, Sue thinks I am perpetually out to lunch, but it was nice to be together without quarreling.

When we got back home, I began my study by asking Sue to list all the things about me that irritate her. I expected her to think it over, perhaps straining to come up with an answer, but she responded immediately.

"You get on my nerves all the time," Sue said. "You are the only person I know who can look busy every day and do nothing."

This rubbed me the wrong way. "That's a great skill," I replied defensively. "Not everyone could pull it off."

This rubbed Sue the wrong way. "You go upstairs and sit in your office for a while, then you take a shower," she said. "Or you go outside and putz around, then you come back in and take a shower. By then, it's cocktail time and you've done nothing."

"All that putzing and showering can build up a thirst," I said.

Then I asked Sue if I have any good points. This time she didn't respond immediately. Finally, she said, "When I give you a list of chores, you do them. Only recently did you take the initiative to do the laundry. You do empty the dishwasher and I don't even have to tell you. And you do vacuum the house. You're always very proud of yourself and I have to say, 'Good job, dear,' and that makes both of us happy."

Sue admitted that I don't always do nothing and added, "You do have a lot of positives. You are caring and loving and you're always good for a laugh. And you're a great father. I love you, dear," said Sue, who asked me what it is about her that rubs me the wrong way.

I could think of only one thing. "You don't put the cap back on the toothpaste," I said. "Even on those tubes with the attached tops, you never snap them shut. Then you put the tube face down on the vanity, which gets all messed up. It's really annoying."

"I don't care about the stupid toothpaste," Sue shot back. "Deal with it."

Another argument lost. But I saved the day by listing all of Sue's positives, which include being loving, kind, generous, thoughtful and extremely beautiful and sexy. "I love you, too, dear," I said, giving her a kiss. I poured each of us a glass of wine and set the table for a romantic candlelight dinner, even though it was still light out.

Sue had the rest of the chicken salad sandwich she couldn't finish at lunch and I had some leftover chicken wings that had been in the freezer since the Super Bowl. Afterward, I helped her do the dishes.

That night, just before bed, Sue left the cap off the toothpaste again. I didn't let it get on my nerves. Now that's the real secret of a long and happy marriage.

"The Honeymooners"

Every three decades, like clockwork, Sue and I drop whatever we are doing and go on a trip. Call us impulsive, but we hadn't been away together, just the two of us, to a place with postcards and palm trees, since our honeymoon in Hawaii in 1978. So we celebrated our 30th anniversary with a week in Barbados.

Sue and I decided not to go to Europe because the dollar is even weaker than I am and the only foreign language I speak is Pig Latin. With the help of a travel agent named Lisa, who suggested Barbados because it offers both fun and relaxation, Sue booked us at the Turtle Beach Resort in Christ Church.

Turtle Beach, so named because it is on a beach and has turtles, though not actually in the hotel itself, which would really slow up room service, is an "all-inclusive" resort. This means you pay a very reasonable price (in our case, about $3,500) for all your food, cocktails and hotel-sponsored activities for the week, in addition to your room and airfare. The deal enables you to eat, drink and be merry for what seems like nothing. Ever since we got back, I have had the uneasy feeling that somebody is going to show up at our house and demand more money.

That won't happen because American currency is worth half of its Barbadian counterpart, so why would anyone want it?

The first thing Sue and I discovered about Barbados is that the residents, called Bajans, pride themselves on two things: Rihanna, the Grammy Award-winning singer, and being the nicest people in the world. They are, in fact, so nice that if you challenge them on this, they will be too nice to argue the point. Except if you challenge them on Rihanna.

The second thing we discovered is that because of the heavy British influence (Barbados is a former British colony and most of the tourists are British), the people drive on the wrong side of the road. They make up for it by politely obeying the rules. This includes going the speed limit and yielding to other drivers at roundabouts, or rotaries, which are so prevalent that the roads must be maintained by the Rotary Club.

That was evident on a shopping excursion to Bridgetown, the capital, which is composed primarily of banks and, to the dismay of visiting husbands, jewelry stores.

The van from the hotel was packed, so I sat next to the driver, Martin Grimes, a 41-year-old family man who is studying to be a minister at Barbados Bible College and has been driving professionally for 20 years.

"I'll drive," I suggested.

"Where are you from?" Grimes asked.

"I was born and raised in Stamford, Connecticut," I said, "but I now live on Long Island, New York."

"You're from New York?" he shrieked. "You people are crazy. You drive on the wrong side of the road. You'll get us all killed."

During the ride, I found out that, like every Bajan I spoke with, Grimes has relatives in the tri-state area.

"Where do people from Barbados go on vacation?" I inquired.

Grimes said, "New York."

Speaking of getting killed, I nearly ended up in Davy Jones's locker, which would have ruined his gym clothes, when I took a surfing lesson. This was not the fault of my instructor, Amra McDowall, who has been surfing for half his life. He is 17.

"I usually teach little kids and teenagers, so you are definitely the oldest student I have ever had," Amra said. "But I know you can do it."

I got a similar vote of confidence from two of Amra's other students, Jamie Tarallo, 16, and his brother, Cory, 14, who were vacationing with their parents, Dawn and Nick Tarallo of Bedford, New York.

"Take your time and don't stand up too fast," Cory said.

Jamie added, "And don't get sand up your nose."

That would have been the least of my problems. I was so bad that I couldn't even stay on the board while paddling out.

"You're wearing too much sunscreen. It's making you slide off," said Amra, who suggested I put on a T-shirt. It didn't work.

Finally, after I made it out a fair distance, Amra had me turn around and try to catch a wave. I remembered Cory's advice about not standing up too fast, except I couldn't stand up at all. The board flipped and hit me on the head. Fortunately, I didn't break it (the board, that is; my head is too thick to be damaged).

This continued for half an hour, after which I trudged back to the beach.

"Don't worry," Amra said consolingly. "Sometimes it takes older people a lot of years to learn."

"I don't have a lot of years left," I said as I thanked him for trying to make a surfer out of me.

I wanted to be the epitome of the surfing mantra "hang 10, dude." Sadly, I couldn't even hang one. I went from dude to dud. At least I didn't get sand up my nose.

Since I had water on the brain, I signed up to go snorkeling with sea turtles, even though turtles don't need snorkels.

Sue and I boarded a catamaran called the Wildcat 1, which was captained by Michael Fedee, 35, who had stocked plenty of rum, the national drink of Barbados, for the dozen guests on board. Fedee and Rico Blackman, 18, the first mate, drank soda.

We anchored in Payne's Bay and slipped into the warm water, which was so clear you could easily see 15 feet to the bottom. Immediately, we were surrounded by greenback turtles, the largest of which, named George, was 4 feet long and weighed about 400 pounds. He introduced himself by letting me shake his flipper. In Barbados, even the turtles are nice.

The highlight of the week came on the last night, when Sue and I had dinner at our own private table on the beach. It was arranged for our anniversary by Sherrie-Ann Waldron, the hotel's guest relations officer.

In fact, everyone at Turtle Beach – including Charles, Racquel, Hermanius, Kim, Wayde, Beyanker, Melissa and Petra – was wonderful.

Sue and I had such a good time that we may go back next year instead of waiting another three decades. At this rate, it will take that long for me to learn how to surf.

"Move Over, Don Juan"

In my dreams, which occur every night and even during the day while I am at work, I often picture myself as a hot-blooded Latin lover. I have hesitated to admit this publicly because I am afraid not only that Antonio Banderas will sue me, but that Sue will laugh and say, "In your dreams."

Now I know I am a regular Don Juan. That's because I have been classified as "the universal romantic" in a study on Mexican food.

The study, which was conducted by my favorite mad scientist, Dr. Alan Hirsch, director of the Smell & Taste Treatment and Research Foundation in Chicago, explored the relationship between Mexican food preference, personality and romantic capability.

According to the methodology, "2,621 literate, English-speaking adults in the U.S. were queried regarding basic demographic as well as Mexican food hedonics." Among the participants, 71 percent were women and 29 percent were men. Seventy-three percent were married.

The food preferences were as follows: tacos, 31 percent; quesadillas, 26 percent; burritos, 22 percent; taco salad, 9 percent; chips and salsa, 8 percent; and nachos, 4 percent.

I may not be in the most popular group, but I am in the best because burritos are my favorite Mexican food and, according to the study, people who prefer burritos are "dramatic, they love being the center of attention. Craving novelty, excitement and stimulation, they are seductive and flirtatious in romance and gregarious, witty and charming in social situations." They also are described as "the universal romantic, compatible with everyone."

"This is great news for your love life," Hirsch said when I called him to discuss the study. "You are such a romantic that your wife will never leave you."

I decided to put our compatibility to the test when I took Sue to a Mexican restaurant called Cinco de Mayo, which means either "sink full of mayonnaise" or "the fifth of May," I am not sure which because in high school and college I took ocho anos de Espanol and I still can't hold a decent conversation.

The only phrases I know are "Cerveza fria, por favor" ("Cold beer, please") and "Donde es el bano?" ("Where is the bathroom?").

Fortunately, there was no communication problem with our waiter, Marcel Salazar, 40, a handsome charmer who was born in Acapulco, Mexico.

"What can I get for you, mi amigo?" he asked me after Sue and I had studied the menu.

"I'll have the burrito supreme because I am the universal romantic," I said. Marcel smiled and replied, "I can tell." Then he asked Sue, "What will you have, senora?"

Sue ordered a chicken quesadilla. According to the Mexican food study, people who prefer quesadillas are "dependable and true friends" and "the rock and driving force in the relationship." As for romance, "Quesadilla lovers are most compatible with those who prefer tacos."

When I explained the Mexican food study to Marcel, he smiled at Sue and said, "I like tacos."

I thought, "Uh-oh."

Luckily for me, Marcel, a divorced father of two, has a girlfriend. Besides, he said, "I prefer fajitas," which weren't in the food study.

I don't know if he was looking for a big tip or what, but Marcel said he could see why I am the universal romantic. "You are very charming and easygoing and you have a good sense of humor, which women like," he said.

As for Sue, Marcel said, "She is muy bonita – very beautiful." Sue blushed.

"Food preference doesn't really matter because you two are already compatible," Marcel said. "I can see that you are very happy together, which is muy importante."

"Si," I said.

It turned out to be a very romantic dinner. The food was delicious and the service was fabulous. The margaritas helped, too.

Unfortunately, I was a little short of cash, so Sue paid the bill and left Marcel a nice tip. But I did go outside in the rain to get the car, which I drove to the front of the restaurant so Sue wouldn't get wet.

When it comes to love, just call me Senor Romance.

"Disorder in the Court"

I have been admitted to many bars in my life (and I've been thrown out of a few, too), but because I didn't go to law school, I never took the bar exam to be a lawyer. That's why I have to plead nolo contendere (a legal term meaning "your fly is open") to being mistaken for an attorney when I accompanied Sue to traffic court.

Let the record show that Sue, also known as the defendant, Susan P. Zezima, represented by Jerry Zezima, received a criminal summons to appear in Lake Grove Village Court on the charge of having an uninspected vehicle sticker on her car.

In this landmark case, People of the State of New York v. Susan P. Zezima, Case No. 06120082, the summons read: "Accusatory instruments filed with this court charge you with the charge(s) shown above. Therefore, you are ordered to appear in person before this Court for arraignment. Failure to appear on the arraignment date shown will result in a warrant for your arrest."

"I'm not a criminal!" the defendant screamed into the phone when she called the court after receiving the summons in the mail. That, of course, would be for the justice system to decide. And the evidence seemed overwhelming: The defendant had been given a ticket for failing to have her car inspected. Her defense: She did, indeed, have it inspected, albeit two days after getting the ticket, but had failed to notify the court of said inspection. Now she was a wanted woman.

It was up to me, in my first case, to clear her good name. This naturally made the defendant nervous because I'm lucky I'm not in jail myself.

Off the record, I showed up merely to offer moral support to my wife. In a calculated effort to sway the judge, I was nattily attired because Sue's original attorney, Natalie Attired, couldn't make it. I wore a crisp blue shirt along with a jacket and tie. I also wore pants because, to tell the truth, the whole truth and nothing but the truth, I don't own a pair of court briefs.

When Sue arrived at the courthouse, accompanied by yours truly, she had to register with a woman who was taking attendance. "Are you her lawyer?" the woman asked me. Before I could answer, Sue said, "He's my husband." The woman didn't see Sue's name on the docket, so she sent us to the court clerk's office. The clerk found Sue's name and said her case would be heard. Then he asked me, "Are you her lawyer?" Before Sue could answer, I said, "I'm her husband."

We sat among the 40 or so other alleged scofflaws who were waiting to have their cases heard. One of them, a man named Jeff, said to me, "Are you her lawyer?" Sue and I, in unison, identified me as her husband.

The district attorney and the assistant district attorney, both of whom were beautiful young women, just like on "Law & Order," asked, "Are you her lawyer?" I was going to say yes but figured I'd be charged with perjury or lying to a grand jury or some other offense and, as a result, be disbarred. So I said, "I'm the defendant's husband."

Everyone at the courthouse thought I was an attorney. I don't know who should have been more insulted, me or the legal profession.

"All rise!" the court clerk announced as the judge, the Honorable Scott D. Middleton, Village Justice, entered the courtroom. Sue looked scared, so I tried to put her at ease with the best legal advice I could think of: "Plead insanity."

In the disposition of the cases before him, Judge Middleton showed a good disposition. He was fair and, as his title implied, honorable. He did, however, go by the letter of the law, so when he fined Jeff $100 for a parking violation, I became concerned for my client.

When Sue's name was called, she rose and approached the bench. I rose, too. "Are you her lawyer?" Judge Middleton asked.

I replied, "I'm Exhibit Z, Your Honor."

"He's my husband," Sue explained.

The assistant DA motioned to me to sit down.

In a moment, it was all over. The judge dismissed Sue's case, meaning she didn't have to pay a fine and her record was clean. Justice was served.

If I do say so myself, Perry Mason couldn't have done better.

"Putting on Heirs"

"I, Jerry Zezima, being of unsound mind and decrepit body, hereby bequeath to my wife, Sue, all of my worldly possessions, including my Three Stooges videos, the six-pack of beer in the refrigerator and all the loose change on the top of my bureau."

That is how I wanted my last will and testament to be worded, with slight variations in case I finished the beer before I died. But because my financial situation had changed in the two decades since I signed my first will and testament, I knew I would need legal advice. So I decided to bite the bullet, which could have made me a habeas corpse, and hire a lawyer.

Sue and I engaged the services of Charlie Brennan, an avuncular gentleman of 75 who has been practicing law for 50 years. "Practice makes perfect, so I'm bound to get it right sooner or later," Charlie said as we sat in his office to discuss my demise (I want a second opinion) and what will happen (probably a big party) after I am gone.

We had the same discussion about Sue, who is convinced that she will go before I do and that I will become a crushing burden to Katie and Lauren, even though they would describe me that way now.

"Do you have any concerns about your children?" Charlie asked.

"Yes," I said. "I want them to support me in my old age."

"It's not going to happen," said Charlie, a widower who has two children and three grandchildren. "My son and daughter are both marvelous, but they would have a tough time pulling the plug. They want me to live to be 107."

"My kids want me to live to be 55," I told Charlie.

"How old are you now?" he inquired.

"Fifty-four," I answered.

Charlie said I should have something known as "per stirpes."

"It sounds like a disease," I said. "And if I had it, Sue would kill me, so I guess I'd need a will anyway."

According to Charlie, "per stirpes" means "to my children" in Latin. "It shows that you won't forget them," he said.

"How could I?" I replied. "Practically all the money I have ever made has gone to my children."

"And now they'll get even more," said Charlie, who told us the story of a client with a secret past. "This couple came in to make out their wills and when the subject came to heirs, I asked them about any children from prior marriages," he recalled. "They said there were none. The next day, the wife called me to say she did have another child her husband didn't know about. That's not the case here, is it?"

Sue and I assured Charlie that we didn't have any other children, although we did ask him to put our dog and cats in our wills, just to make sure our daughters would take good care of them in case any of the pets survived us.

"They'd live better than we would," I said. Sue agreed.

We also discussed living wills and what would happen if I became incoherent. "Can I collect now?" Sue wondered.

And we talked about organ donations. "I can't play the organ, although I was once the guest triangle player in a symphony orchestra," I said, adding that I planned to leave my brain to science. Sue said it might lead to a cure for stupidity.

When the subject of burial came up, I said, "I'd like an open casket, but I want to be turned around so my feet are showing. That way everyone could remark on how good I looked."

Afterward, as Sue watched me sign my will, my head was filled with the strains of a very worrisome song: "The Merry Widow."

These are tough things to discuss, but they have to be faced, and Sue and I couldn't have picked a better person for the job than Charlie, who not only gives lawyers a good name, but who loves what he does and doesn't plan to retire because, he said, in a shameful admission for an attorney, "I don't play golf."

As Sue and I left, Charlie wished us many more years of life together.

"Thanks," I said. "Where there's a will, there's a way."

"High Roller"

I am so bad at games of chance that I was once beaten in blackjack by my dog, so I never thought I would be a high roller at a casino. In fact, I had never been to a casino until I visited Mohegan Sun in Uncasville, Connecticut, where I defied the odds, despite being a bit odd myself, by hitting the jackpot on a slot machine and pocketing a grand total of $11.50.

My bonanza was the icing on the cake of Sue and my mother, whose shared birthday was being celebrated with a trip to the aforementioned gaming emporium. The party included my father; Katie and Dave; Lauren, and my sisters, Elizabeth and Susan, all of whom had been there before but did not, in case the IRS is reading this, come home in a higher tax bracket.

The first thing I noticed about Mohegan Sun was that it is roughly the size of Rhode Island, which it is near and might invade after a planned expansion. The main difference between the two places is that the casino has both a surplus and a roof.

So it was not surprising that I did what a great many people (including some of those I was with) have been telling me to do for years: I got lost. I must have spent half the day wandering aimlessly, calling or receiving cell-phone calls from everyone except my father, who wisely doesn't have a cell phone. They were all wondering where the hell I was. One time I said: "Rhode Island." It didn't help.

Shortly after we arrived, I spotted a pleasant-looking, grandmotherly lady sitting at a slot machine. She looked like she knew what she was doing, so I went over and sat down next to her, hoping some of her expertise would translate into beginner's luck for me.

"I just hit the jackpot for $750!" she announced excitedly before identifying herself as Frances Ruzzi of Poughkeepsie, New York. Not only was she indeed a pleasant grandmother, but she was celebrating her 86th birthday with her family, including her daughter, Donna Yantorno of Danbury, Connecticut, who noted that her mom is a casino veteran.

"We're celebrating my wife's and my mother's birthday," I said. "Maybe it's a good omen." Then I asked Frances, as she kindly allowed me to call her, about her secret of gambling success. She smiled and said, "I have no idea."

"Neither do I," I said. "It's my first time in a casino."

"I bet you'll win," Frances said. "Good luck."

I got up and, as visions of moneybags danced in my head, promptly got lost.

Eventually I met up with everyone for a late lunch, followed by a round of cocktails to toast the birthday girls. Then it was time to see if I could break the bank.

I accompanied Dave, the best gambler in the family, to a craps table and, as I watched him lose $80, found out how the game got its name. Figuring I would lose my shirt, not to mention my pants, in which I had only $25, I didn't even bother playing and instead went over to the blackjack tables. Two things prevented me from getting into a game:

1. Most of the tables had a minimum opening wager of $25.

2. My dog, Lizzie, defeated me in a tournament we played at home one night. It's a good thing we weren't playing for money.

So I went over to a roulette wheel with Dave and won the first game before losing the next two. The only thing left to try was a slot machine. I found one next to Catherine Mitchell, a retiree from Warwick, Rhode Island. Like me, she was making her casino debut. "I just lost $200," said the mother of 10 and grandmother of 13. "I'm never coming back."

This did not bode well. Neither did the fact that Sue and Lauren, whom I found at another bank of machines, hadn't won anything. I put some money in the one-armed bandit and used one arm of my own to pull the lever. Then I pulled it again. And again. By the time I was done, I had won $11.50.

I took my ticket to the redemption window and handed it to a cashier named Dora. "Do you have a wheelbarrow so I can cart away all this money?" I asked. Dora didn't even smile. She handed me two fives, a one and a couple of quarters. Then she put a sign on the counter that said: "NEXT WINDOW, PLEASE."

I felt like a high roller until Sue pointed out that I had spent $25 to make $11.50, which means I actually lost $13.50. I'd love to go back to the casino, but maybe I should quit while I'm behind.

"Home, Sweat Home"

In the 10 years since Sue and I bought our house, which the bank actually owns but kindly allows us to pay for, I have come to realize that home is where the heartburn is.

In fact, I am having chest pains just thinking about all the work I have done around the house over the past decade.

Because Sue and I spent the first 20 years of our marriage in either an apartment or a condominium, I was pathetically ill-equipped to be a homeowner. I had such limited knowledge of tools that I thought a screwdriver was vodka and orange juice. I don't even want to tell you what I thought a hoe was.

"But now," Sue said the other evening at dinner, as we marked a decade in our dream house, which occasionally gives me nightmares, "you're getting better, although you still have a lot to learn. Like how to use a power washer."

She was referring, unfortunately, to my latest failed project, which began that morning when I went to a home improvement center to rent a machine that a sales associate named Fred started on the first try.

When I got the thing home, of course, it wouldn't start, which was all right with me because I would have had to climb a ladder to wash the upper part of the house. We have a Colonial that is high enough to give a mountain goat nosebleeds and I am afraid of being any higher off the ground than the top of my head.

So I brought the power washer back. Fred easily started it again.

If I am good at anything, Sue said, it's mowing the lawn. "You do that well," she acknowledged. "It's one job you have perfected. At least you don't get frustrated and swear and throw things like you used to."

That's because it's hard to throw a lawn mower. But I do like to cut the grass because it gives me an excuse not to go inside to paint.

Every painting project has been a brush with disaster. Since we moved in, I have painted 20 times, which amounts to two projects per year. The worst was when I painted the living room for the second time. I had to pull down three huge ceiling beams that Sue said, after I had painted the room the first time, she didn't like.

One beam almost came crashing down on my head. All three left holes that I had to plug up before I painted. Fortunately, Sue is only 5-foot-1, so she thinks the ceiling looks good.

Last year, after I painted our bedroom for the second time, I announced my retirement from painting. "You're not retired," Sue said the other evening. "You're just on hiatus."

Great. She probably wants me to paint the downstairs bathroom again. I have already painted it three times.

Speaking of bathrooms, we once had to hire a contractor to gut and refurbish all of them, including the two full baths upstairs. When they were finished, I had to paint them.

Two years ago, when Katie was engaged to be married, Sue suggested we have the bridal shower at our house because, she reasoned, "We'll save money." Then she announced that the kitchen had to be redone. We hired another contractor. We didn't save money.

To make matters worse, our underground oil tank ruptured a week before the shower. The side yard had to be dug up and an old, rusty, above-ground tank was temporarily placed on the lawn in full sight of the guests. The tank was festooned with balloons and a sign that read: "Congratulations!"

The kitchen was finished the day before the shower. We had it wallpapered, so at least I didn't have to paint again.

In the past 10 years, I have learned that a house is not a home unless there is something to do. And there always is. In fact, my next project is cleaning out the garage, which is filled with boxes that haven't been opened since we moved in.

Frankly, I'd rather power wash the house.

"Color My World"

Because I have more gray matter on the outside of my head than I do on the inside, I am often asked why I don't dye my hair. "I do," I always respond. "I dye it gray so I'll seem more mature." To which people invariably say, "It's not working."

So when my barber, Maria Vieira, recently told me about a new kind of hair coloring treatment that covers enough of the gray to make you look younger but not enough so people will think you put shoe polish on your head, I decided to go for it. This wasn't just because my cranium resembled a snow-capped mountain peak, which could be why I frequently had brain freeze and was considered over the hill, but also because I wanted to see if anyone would notice that some of the snow melted.

As I sat in a chair at Charmed Salon & Spa in Miller Place, New York, Maria confirmed my theory that very few people, young or old, know what their original hair color was.

"They range from teenagers who have already dyed their hair a dozen times to seniors who went gray years ago," said Maria, who admitted that she can't remember exactly what color her hair used to be. It's now a rich brown with blond highlights and looks, if I do say so, beautiful. I was hoping she could make me look the same. Or at least young enough so Boy Scouts wouldn't start offering to help me cross the street.

But first, Katie McConnach, Maria's assistant, put color block along my hairline, my sideburns and the back of my neck. "We don't want to color your ears," she said. Then she put some of the stuff around my mustache, which looked like a giant Brillo pad and also had to be dyed.

Next, Maria rubbed Menz Natural Hair Color Gel by Scruples into my curly locks, which she said were very thick. "So is my skull," I replied. Maria didn't disagree, although she did say that she was giving me a light ash brown color. "I know it's your natural shade because you still have brown in the back," she noted. "Besides, it will keep you lightheaded."

Then she got a paintbrush and applied the gel to my mustache and my eyebrows, after which she set a timer for five minutes. I felt like an egg.

Fortunately, the yolk wasn't on me. After the timer went off and the gel had been rinsed out, I looked in the mirror and saw a younger but not entirely different me. "Now you have more pepper in your salt," said Maria, adding: "Let's see if anyone notices."

The first test came when Sue arrived home. It was a Friday afternoon and I helped her carry in some groceries, after which I talked with her in the kitchen. She looked right at me. "Wow," I thought, "she can't tell."

Later on, Katie and Dave, who live in Boston, came down for the weekend. Neither one said anything about my hair.

The next day, we all saw Lauren, for whom hair is a way of life. You'd need a calculator to figure out all the different shades of blond and brown she has colored it. She is very hair-aware, yet she failed to notice that I had colored mine.

On Sunday morning, before Katie and Dave left, I gathered them and Sue in the family room and asked if they noticed anything different about me. "You look thinner," Katie said. Sue and Dave were stumped. When I said I had colored my hair, Sue, who colors hers, said, "I've been married to you for 31 years and I didn't even notice." Katie, a journalist who colors her hair, said, "I feel terrible because it's my job to notice things." Dave, also a journalist (he doesn't color his hair), said, "I thought your mustache looked a little darker, but I didn't want to say anything."

That afternoon, I asked Lauren, who had come over with her friend Jen, if she noticed anything different about me. "I saw you in the sunlight before and thought your hair looked browner," she said. "Did you color it?" I said yes and added that it took her, a hair goddess, two days to catch on. Jen said, "It's very natural."

So now I look younger but still distinguished, if no more mature. It was an experience to dye for.

"Grape Expectations"

My favorite Latin phrase, which must have been translated improperly when I was in high school, is "Veni, vidi, vino." It means, "I came, I saw, I drank a lot of wine."

That is what I have been saying since I introduced my very own merlot.

Actually, the wine has just been introduced by Castello di Borghese, the oldest vineyard on Long Island, and it's called Borghese 2004 Reserve Merlot. But I can say with great pride, a pleased palate and a slight buzzing in my ears that I helped to make it.

Since wine needs time to age (I don't because I get more decrepit every day), the process began in 2002, when I drove out to Castello di Borghese and, with the permission of the owners, Marco and Ann Marie Borghese, picked a bunch of cabernet franc grapes so I could take them home to make my own wine.

Back at Chateau de Zezima, I decided to re-create the famous scene in "I Love Lucy" in which Lucille Ball crushes wine grapes with her feet. I put my grapes in the bathtub, removed my shoes and socks, and stomped away. Then I plopped the crushed grapes into a stainless steel pot, covered them and let them ferment. A week later, I strained the mess, poured the juice into an empty wine bottle, which I capped with a party balloon to trap the vapors and prevent the house from blowing up, and let it ferment for another week.

When I took my wine, which I dubbed Cabernet Jerry 2002, back to Castello di Borghese, the winemaker took one sip and spluttered, "It tastes like nail polish remover!"

After assuring me that my feet were not responsible for the disaster, he took me down to the cellar so I could help make real wine. This required me to again take off my shoes and socks, put on a T-shirt and a pair of swim trunks, and climb through a small porthole leading to the inside of a 3,000-gallon stainless steel tank containing four tons of thick, soggy merlot grape skins.

My job was to stand knee-deep in the bone-chilling gunk and, using an orange plastic shovel, dump the skins into an auger-driven pump that funneled them into a 900-gallon press. After a fermentation process that would last slightly longer than the two weeks it took to make my cabernet, the result would be the 2004 Reserve Merlot.

Slow forward to 2009. Sue and I, along with Katie and Dave, who were visiting for the weekend, drove out to the vineyard to see if my merlot was ready.

"You're in luck," said Marco Borghese. "We're just coming out with it now."

Although the label year is 2004, Marco explained, "Wine has to stay in barrels for at least three years and in bottles for as long as you want."

Since the winery has been voted best vineyard on Long Island, I had no doubt that Marco knew the proper time to come out with my merlot. "It's not our very finest," he acknowledged. "And it's not because of your feet. Still," added Marco, who gave me a bottle with his compliments, "I hope you enjoy it."

At home, I opened the bottle and, like a true oenophile, took a whiff of the cork. It smelled like cork. Then I poured some of my merlot into glasses for Sue, Katie, Dave and yours truly. I took a sip, let the wine sit on the back of my tongue and swallowed. "Magnifique," I announced.

"It's good," Sue said. "Very peppery."

"And sharp," Katie added.

Dave said, "I smell pepper. No feet as yet. Very good."

My merlot had passed the family test, but what would a professional wine critic say? To find out, I asked my pal Peter M. Gianotti, a respected food and wine critic for Newsday, to give me his unbiased opinion.

Because there are no wine glasses in the office, Peter used a paper cup. "It's plummy," he said after taking a sip. "And it has a back bite.

It might need a little more time in the bottle, but I would have it with pizza."

The ultimate compliment! What more could a winemaker want? I don't know how you say it in Latin, but I do know that, if she were still around, Lucy would be proud.

"Day at the Museum"

Aside from fame, fortune and talent, Ben Stiller has nothing on me. That's because I recently spent a day at the museum.

Yes, it was the American Museum of Natural History in New York City, the site of Stiller's 2006 box office hit, "Night at the Museum." I didn't spend a night at the museum for two good reasons: It closed at 5:45 p.m. and I am not, for better or for worse, Ben Stiller.

Still, Sue and I decided to spend an afternoon at this famous institution, which we hadn't visited since Katie and Lauren were kids about 20 years ago, to see if anything would come alive.

"Oh, wow, things come alive all the time," said Abiba Ouattara, a guard who has been working at the museum for four years. "Especially at night."

Ouattara should know because she sometimes works the night shift. "The dinosaurs are more interesting than Ben Stiller," she said.

"Maybe I could be in an exhibit," I told her. "I'm a fossil."

"No, you're not," replied Ouattara, whose love of her job and delightful sense of humor make her a great ambassador for the museum. "But you could be in the human origin section. That's where we all belong."

Sue and I decided to start with an even older exhibit, in the David H. Koch Dinosaur Wing, which is oddly named because dinosaurs didn't have wings, unless you believe, as do many paleontologists, that they were closely related to birds, especially on their mother's side.

We saw all the biggies, including T. rex (my, what big teeth you have!) and apatosaurus, formerly known as brontosaurus, a name it must have used as an alias to escape meat eaters such as allosaurus, who was there, too.

We also saw stegosaurus, a huge armored creature that had a brain the size of a walnut, making it the congressman of dinosaurs.

"No wonder it's extinct," Sue commented.

"I have a small brain and I'm not extinct," I said.

"No," Sue noted, "not yet."

All the dinosaurs died out tens of millions of years ago from one of three causes: climate change, a comet that hit Earth or, as cartoonist Gary Larson theorized in a famous "Far Side" strip, smoking.

Even though the skeleton crew didn't come alive, it was great to see them again. But an even bigger thrill awaited in a new exhibit called "Extreme Mammals," of which I, of course, am one.

Just as I knew the names of all the dinosaurs when I was a kid because I was, and still am, an encyclopedia of useless information, I also was familiar with the prehistoric mammals, including the woolly mammoth, the saber-toothed tiger (not really a tiger, but it's dead, so why quibble?) and the giant ground sloth. All of them were here, as was a gigantic hornless rhinoceros named Indricotherium, the largest land mammal that ever lived. It was even bigger than Orson Welles before he, too, became extinct.

Sue and I also made it to the human origin section, where I spotted many of my ancestors, who could easily be distinguished from me because none of them, even the women, had a mustache.

The museum is so large and so fascinating that no one could possibly see it all in one day. Or even one night, as Martin Hollander, a volunteer at the information desk, told me. There is, indeed, a "Night at the Museum" program, but it's for kids 8-12 years old.

"You'd have to bring a brat," Hollander said.

"I'm a brat. And intellectually, I'm about 8," I said. "Could my wife bring me?"

"Yes," Hollander replied. "You could be Benjamin Button."

Unfortunately, I couldn't be Ben Stiller. But if he doesn't want to star in another "Night at the Museum" movie, I'll gladly take his place.

"Moby-Sick"

Call me Ishmael. Call me captain. But don't call me seasick.

That's more than I could say for most of the 80 people – including Sue – who went out on a boat to watch whales but instead, in a stunning display of mass disgorgement that even Herman Melville couldn't have imagined, gave new meaning to the old whaling term "Thar she blows!"

Our high-seas adventure began aboard the Viking Starship, a 140-foot-long vessel out of Montauk, New York. Under the able command of the friendly and experienced crew – Capt. Joseph DiLiberto, mate Alex Georgiev and naturalist Artie Kopelman – the Starship set sail at 9:30 a.m. on a six-hour tour, a six-hour tour (sorry, "Gilligan's Island" fans) about 15 miles into the Atlantic. Destination: the feeding grounds of majestic marine mammals, including the fin whale, the second-largest species, which can grow to 80 feet in length.

Before Sue and I boarded, I noticed a sign on the dock next to the ship. It read: "No firearms allowed onboard." Now I know why: If you get violently sick out on the water, you'll want to shoot yourself.

A storm had passed offshore the night before and the morning broke cloudy and chilly, but the conditions, if not ideal, weren't bad enough to cancel the trip.

Kopelman stood on deck with a microphone as the boat chugged out of the harbor and, in a funny and informative routine that included fascinating facts about the creatures we hoped to see, explained what we should do in the event of seasickness. Ill passengers should not use bags but should go "over the rail," Kopelman said, adding: "And not into the wind."

The first sign of trouble came about five miles out, just past the Montauk Point Lighthouse, where the Viking Starship acted more like the Jefferson Starship: It was rocking and rolling in the increasingly churning ocean. Several people, who had turned greener than the water, clutched the rail. Others, disregarding Kopelman's instructions, clutched bags. Sue clutched me.

Apparently, I was the only passenger, in addition to a group of little kids, who was having a good time. It was like being at an amusement park except that no one else thought it was amusing.

Among the afflicted was Sue, who got sick five times. It may have been a record. At one point, I went inside to get her some napkins and spoke with Kobi Kobayashi, who runs the snack bar.

"I guess business hasn't been too good today," I said.

Kobayashi shook his head and replied, "I made three breakfasts – sausage and eggs – but they probably went over the side."

Kobayashi, a former commercial fisherman from Japan, has also been a filmmaker. He was the cinematographer on the 1977 Oscar winner for best short documentary, "I'll Find a Way."

"If you made a movie about this trip," I noted, "you could call it 'I'll Find a Wave.' A lot of people have." Kobayashi didn't disagree.

About 12 miles out, Capt. Joe decided to cut the trip short and turn around. "It's too bad," he said, "because we've had an 80 percent success rate this year. We've been out 20 times and have seen whales 16 times. None today, though."

"Maybe they're sick, too," I suggested.

"Seasickness is mostly mind over matter," said Capt. Joe, adding that he used to get sick as a boy when he went on fishing trips with his father and uncles. "You grow out of it."

On the way back in, the water had calmed considerably, so Capt. Joe let me take the wheel. For five minutes, under strict supervision, I was Capt. Jerry.

About half an hour later, after the real captain docked the boat under sunny skies, Sue and I, along with scores of ashen-faced, wobbly-legged, would-be whale watchers, disembarked. I was going to ask Sue if she wanted to get some clams for lunch, but I didn't want to end up sleeping with the fishes.

"Identity Crisis"

In the immortal words of Popeye, I am what I am. Unfortunately, what I am can't be printed here. I don't even know who I am anymore. That's because my identity was stolen.

I never thought this would happen because you'd have to be crazy to want to be me. Even if you were caught and went to trial, you could easily get off, either by pleading insanity or by claiming the cops had the wrong man. Then I'd get arrested.

In contrast to the old Sammy Davis Jr. song "I've Gotta Be Me," I don't want to be myself. It's a terrible predicament, but there's nothing I can do about it.

Despite the prospect of being married to someone richer and a lot more interesting, Sue decided to do something about it when she noticed charges on my debit card for $1.13.

"Is that all I'm worth?" I asked. "What an insult!"

"There are three charges," Sue pointed out, "so you're worth $3.39."

That made me feel a little better, but I still couldn't understand why anyone would want to steal my identity, especially since I had to take a vow of poverty when I went into journalism.

In fact, my life is lived in increments of $20 because I use my debit card almost exclusively at the ATM, which in my case stands for Abominable Transaction Machine. I usually withdraw $20 so I can put enough gas in my car to go to work so I can earn enough money to put gas in my car to go to work. At least I have a job. Then again, if I didn't, I wouldn't have to put gas in my car.

At any rate, Sue called the bank to find out what was going on and spoke with a very nice customer representative named Renee, who wanted to speak with me because those little charges were being put on my card.

"Someone is probably downloading songs on an iPod," Renee said.

"I don't have an iPod or iTunes, although I do have iTeeth," I told her. "I'm not technologically advanced."

"Neither am I," said Renee, adding that she would put a block on my card but that I would have to go to a bank branch to get a new one.

A little while later, Sue and I were sitting in the office of Friday McGraw, a small-business specialist who is as terrific as his name.

"Identity theft is a big problem," said Friday, which also happened to be the day we were there. "I've already done three this morning." Then he handed me a pair of scissors and asked if I wanted to cut up my card.

"I've always been a cutup, so why not?" I said. Friday looked on as I snipped away. "Wow!" I chirped. "I'm literally performing plastic surgery!"

"I guess you don't do that for a living," Friday commented. "You're too excited." He also said that identity thieves typically put small charges on a card at first. If the card holder doesn't do anything about it, the thieves will then put on charges that could total thousands of dollars.

In trying to figure out where the theft might have occurred, Friday asked, "Where was the last place you ate?"

"My parents' house," I replied, explaining that we had stayed overnight.

"If your identity got stolen there, you're in trouble," said Friday, who has helped my parents with their banking and knows they're honest people.

"Still," I wondered, "why would anyone want it?"

"I guess there's at least one idiot out there," Friday answered with a smile. He issued me a temporary card, changed the number on our checking account, arranged for me to get a new debit card and new checks, and otherwise handled the whole transaction with great professionalism and good humor.

"Now you can be you again," he said.

"It's small consolation," I replied. "But at least I can put gas in my car."

"Mr. and Mrs. Excitement"

I don't want to bore you with tales of my marital exploits, although I don't see why this column should be different from any other one, but Sue and I are anything but boring. In 31 years of wedded bliss, we have led the most exciting lives that two people who haven't done much can possibly lead. This includes puttering around the house, sending out for pizza and, the high point of any boomer couple's thrill-packed day, trying to stay awake for the 11 o'clock news.

So when I read a recent study on avoiding boredom in marriage, I fell asleep in a rocking chair in front of the TV and woke up when the news was over. Then I woke up Sue, who was snoozing in an easy chair, and we both went to bed.

The next morning, I went to see the co-author of the study, Dr. Arthur Aron, a professor of psychology at Stony Brook University.

For Aron, who worked on the study with Irene Tsapelas of Stony Brook and Terri Orbuch of the University of Michigan, this was his latest scientific triumph. His previous study showed that brain activity in longtime spouses who are still in love is the same as the brain activity in MRIs of newly romantic couples.

"You could take an MRI of my brain," I told Aron, "but you probably wouldn't find any activity."

"That would mean you are still out of your head in love with your wife," he suggested.

It goes without saying, but I will say it anyway, that Aron is brilliant. He proved it in the boredom study, which was published in Psychological Science, by finding that "couples need to make their lives together more exciting."

Aron knows what he's talking about because he has been married for 35 years to Dr. Elaine Aron, a psychotherapist who is the author of several books, including "The Highly Sensitive Person."

"I'm not bored in my marriage because my wife and I like to go out on little dates," said Aron. "We enjoy doing different things, like finding new places to eat."

"My wife and I do, too," I said.

"Maybe," Aron replied, "my wife and I will run into you and your wife some Saturday night."

If they do, it will probably be at the burger joint that Sue and I recently found. It's actually a neighborhood bar called Reese's 1900 Pub, which is a few miles from another neighborhood bar we also frequent, Billie's 1890 Saloon.

Finding a new place to have delicious burgers and cold beer has added considerable excitement to our marriage. Just the thought of deciding whether to have fried onions or bacon as toppings, or whether to go with cheddar or Swiss cheese, is enough to make us giddy with the spark of first love. Then again, it could be the beer.

Still, like many empty nesters, Sue and I have discovered that it's the little things that prevent boredom from creeping into a marriage. That's because, after putting both of our daughters through college and marrying one of them off, we don't have enough money left for the big things.

True, we went to Barbados last year for our 30th anniversary, the first time we had been away together, just the two of us, to a place with postcards and palm trees, since our honeymoon in Hawaii. We vowed to go back this year but ended up staying home and going to a local beach that did not, I regret to say, have postcards or palm trees, although it did have a snack bar.

Now that the weather is cooler, Sue and I spend our exciting Saturday nights either at home watching rented movies and trying to stay awake to the end or going out on little dates for burgers and beer. And if we should happen to run into Arthur and Elaine Aron, the first round is on them.

"It's in the Bag"

When I was a young father, I learned an important lesson: Parenting is a dirty job, but somebody has to do it. The person who taught me this lesson was Sue, a young mother who believed in the division of labor: If I couldn't go into labor, the least I could do was to change our children's diapers.

The memories of those long-ago days are wafting back to me in pungent waves of nostalgia because I have just read an advertisement for the Magic Bag, a new product from a Los Angeles-based company called Timi & Leslie. The bag has a basketball motif and is supposed to be used by fathers to dispose of their babies' dirty diapers.

"No more skipping diaper duty, Dad," says the ad. "Made of real basketball leather, the vinyl-covered tote has a water-resistant lining, two bottle pockets, a magnetic-snap closure and a matching pad – the better to catch dribble with."

The ad doesn't feature a slogan for the Magic Bag, but I have a suggestion: "It's a slam dump!"

Because of the cost ($155), it's also a long shot.

Still, it's nice that Dad isn't being forgotten, much as he would like to be in this case. But the Magic Bag raises two questions:

1. What if Dad isn't a basketball fan?
2. Will it really help him become the very model of the modern man?

Let's face it, when it comes to diaper detail, most men are babies. They can get their hands dirty doing any number of manly things, from digging up the backyard to working with hazardous materials, but ask them to do a job that mothers perform as easily as breathing (it's actually not a good idea to breathe while doing it) and they cry even more than the kid they have to clean up.

This is not true of all fathers, of course, but if forced to make a choice between changing a diaper and undergoing a root canal without

Novocain, the average man would choose – I hate to admit this – changing a diaper, because if there is one thing guys hate more than poop, it's pain.

Which is another reason why most men are babies.

Because both of my daughters are potty trained (they're in their 20s) and the statute of limitations has run out, meaning I can't be prosecuted for dereliction of duty, so to speak, I can now admit that I have changed only about half a dozen diapers in my life.

Like most young fathers I knew at the time, I would fake it. Here's my confession:

Sue would often go shopping to escape all the smells and messes and crying (she'd want a break from the kids, too) and would leave me in charge. After Katie was born, I'd have one baby to take care of. When Lauren came along a couple of years later, I'd have two.

"Do you know where the bottles are?" Sue would ask.

"Yes," I would reply confidently. "In the liquor cabinet."

Sue would roll her eyes. "Don't forget to feed the girls," she would remind me. "And if they do anything, change their diapers."

Then she would bolt out the door before I had a chance to ask any questions or remember I had an appointment for a root canal.

Everything would be fine because I loved playing with the kids and giving them their bottles. But if they did anything, I'd pretend I didn't notice. It wasn't easy because if Sue was out for the day and one of the kids did something five minutes after she left, I would have to open the windows or, if it was January, hold my breath until either I passed out or the paint began to peel off the walls.

When Sue came home, I would be literally gasping for air. "Whew!" she would say. "Didn't you notice that Katie needs to be changed?" To which I would give my patented response: "She must have just done it."

I am embarrassed to admit this because I feel like a delinquent father. Of course, it's easy for me to say it now because my kids are grown and I don't yet have grandchildren. But when I do, I won't shirk my responsibilities. In fact, I'll do what any proud grandpa would do: I'll buy a Magic Bag for my son-in-law.

EPILOGUE

So here we are, Sue and I, a pair of baby boomers, perched in our empty nest. No, we won't always have Paris, because we have never been there. Mostly, we've been home, first in Stamford, where Sue and I were born and raised and where Katie and Lauren were, too, and now on Long Island, where we await the next chapter in our lives.

We ask ourselves the most common questions asked by people our age: Will we be mother and father of the bride again? Will we be around to hear the pitter-patter of the next generation's little feet? If so, will Grandfather know best? (There is no earthly reason to think the answer to the last question is yes, but it's fun to contemplate.)

The only thing we know for sure is that, for people like Sue and me, this is the best time of life. A boom time for boomers, if you will. And, with luck, as well as more of the same crazy things you have just read about, there are plenty of good times ahead.